This Gift, This Poem

This Gift, This Poem

Edited by
Jean Kent, David Musgrave
Carolyn Rickett and Jen Webb

PUNCHER & WATTMANN

First published by Puncher and Wattmann in 2021
PO Box 279
Waratah NSW 2298

http://www.puncherandwattmann.com
puncherandwattmann@bigpond.com

NATIONAL
LIBRARY
OF AUSTRALIA

A catalogue record for this book is available from the National Library of Australia

ISBN 9781922571168

Cover design by DESIGN & PROSPER
https://designandprosper.co/
Printed by Lightning Source International

We acknowledge the Australian Aboriginal and Torres Strait Islander peoples of this nation as the traditional custodians of the lands on which we write, read and share poetry. We pay our respects to ancestors and Elders, past and present and express our gratitude for their creativity and storytelling.

For Dr Cedric Greive, Professor Jill Gordon,
& the New Leaves poets

Table of Contents

These words (this gift, this poem)
— Rosemary Dobson, 'The Anthropologist'

Preface

At the start of this trail-blazing anthology, I am honoured to share these reflections on behalf of Avondale, Australia's newest University. No doubt, when this collection was first conceived, there was little awareness of the global trauma that would surround us during the COVID-19 pandemic. As I write, millions around the world continue to grapple with the tragedy of a pandemic that stubbornly refuses to disappear. Into this environment comes an anthology of hope, a soothing balm designed to help us pause for a few moments, to breathe deeply and to appreciate the healing that poetry brings. It is indeed a gift.

An increasingly rich vein of research points to the healing power of poetry. This includes research conducted by one of the co-editors of this volume, Associate Professor Carolyn Rickett, who provides significant thought leadership at Avondale University and across the higher education sector. For over 120 years, Avondale University has prioritised a distinctive emphasis on holistic education that encompasses spiritual, physical, intellectual and emotional wellbeing. Our focus on transformational interdisciplinary research has further strengthened our evidence-based approach to health and wellbeing, Christian education and spirituality. Serving our world for good through educational excellence and high impact, applied research is at the heart of Avondale University's purpose; which is why it is such a pleasure to be affiliated with this inspiring anthology. On behalf of Avondale University, I'm particularly pleased to celebrate the creativity of an impressive array of Australian poets whose innovative work attests to the healing comfort of poetry.

As our Avondale University community looks ahead to our future as a new Australian University, I commend this uplifting anthology to you, as a fellow traveller. Together, we have good reason to grasp new challenges, uncertainties and opportunities with hope. In opening this poetry collection, this gift, I wish you healing in pain, respite in sadness, comfort through trauma, connection and wholeness.

Professor Kerri-Lee Krause PhD PFHEA FSRHE
Provost and Senior Deputy Vice Chancellor

Foreword

The poet Robert Frost considered a poem to be 'a momentary stay against confusion'[1]. Wallace Stevens argued that poetry, because of the power of the imagination to transform everyday reality, enables people to cope with the daily grind and numbness of routine. He said that the poet's function 'is to make his imagination ... become the light in the minds of others. His role, in short, is to help people to live their lives.'[2]

Many poets over time have made many statements about poetry. Poetry, like all art forms, has varying approaches: a poem can be dramatic, narrative, epic, epigrammatic, surreal, irrational; it can highlight the structures and forms within language itself; and the lyric poem, because of its musicality, concentration of thought and portrayal of emotion in a formalised way, can bring us into connection with the inner life. A good poem can have an enduring and memorable effect, it invites the reader into new ways of feeling and seeing, to experience how feeling has been animated and given shape.

Poetry provides a unique experience with language which is often intense, elevated, heightened, and I would venture to say 'sacred' in as much as it frames, like a painting or piece of music, moments in time, holding them up and away from the general noise and flux, giving us a reprieve, some greater stillness in which to apprehend and to contemplate. That 'momentary stay against confusion' as Robert Frost so aptly put it. It is useful to remember that poetry emerged out of song, chanting and dance, those acts of ritual, celebration, and worship that attempt to speak of the sacred mystery of experience. When we read a

---

1 Frost, Robert. 'The Figure a Poem Makes' in *Collected Poems*. Henry Holt and Company, New York, 1939.
2 Stevens, Wallace. 'The Noble Rider and the Sound of Words' in *The Necessary Angel: Essays on Reality and Imagination*. Vintage, New York, 1951.

good poem, we give ourselves over to a process of becoming the poem: we enter its rhythms, form, sounds and its flow of images. A poem can quicken our sense of language to the point where we participate most fully in meaning-making. The writer and reader make meaning together. Only in poetry do we encounter language which is awake to its power and potential, to its innate ability to be moving and memorable.

Poetry has always been one of the most powerful and effective forms for addressing and exploring deep human questions. Partly this is because poetry is connected so intimately with the breath. The word 'inspiration' comes from the Latin root meaning 'to breathe upon' or 'to breathe into'. A poem will use tools such as repetition of vowel and consonant sounds, recurrences of words, phrases, sound patterns and images and these act as regulating mechanisms, not only for the breath, but consequently for the movement of thought. Repeated structures have a calming and stilling effect, as in mantra repetition, often allowing the excess noise of the mind to drop away. The poet Edward Hirsch has said that 'repetitions loosen the intellect for reverie'[3]. These specific and concentrated tools of poetry enable a more intense, a more visceral connection with language than say reading a report or a newspaper article, or a menu. It is this connection that poetry has with the body and the senses that gives it its power as a 'felt' experience, as one in which both the body, mind and heart are involved.

A true poem is not simply an accumulation of sense data, but through its tools, especially simile and metaphor, a poem tries to tell us of some lost connection, or it conjures a new one. It is through simile and metaphor that the poet tries to create those sacred spaces, relations between things that formerly might have been unnoticed. Image making is part of our search for meanings that will allow us to feel our place within the larger scheme of things.

---

3 Hirsch, Edward. *How to Read a Poem and Fall in Love with Poetry.* Harcourt Brace and Company, 1999, 22.

A good image opens us up to questioning and to deep-looking: things which seem separate begin to cohere, and in this state there occurs an enlarging of feeling and understanding. The word metaphor comes from a Greek term meaning to 'transfer' or 'carry across.' Poetry is an attempt by the human heart and mind to heal the distance and separation we can sometimes experience, that sense that the world is hidden by appearances, that there is something deeper going on underneath.

Many studies have produced evidence that creativity has a therapeutic effect, that the benefits of writing poetry (and indeed reading it) are cathartic because the poet needs to objectify their feelings and therefore gains distance and perspective on what can seem overwhelming. The function of all art is to engage our intelligence and emotions, to relieve boredom and to reset everyday life by offering us feelings for which we do not have to suffer the consequences. It allows us to love, triumph, hope, despair, dread, condemn, and hate etc. without any of the dangers or effects those feelings might ordinarily produce.

Perhaps one of poetry's most significant benefits and gifts to us is community, that sense we are all connected with each other in our joys and sufferings, the fellowship of human feeling. One of poetry's chief purposes is to draw people together. It has always been a means for communicating stories, beliefs, customs, and values of a people. In moments of crisis, we turn to poetry because it has that unique ability to express and formalise emotion, to bring something of ourselves into being. The English poet Ruth Padel has said, 'everyone has a poetry-shaped hole in them. And though today many people fill this hole with other artefacts like pop music, they often turn to the real thing when the precariousness makes itself intensely felt.'[4] At best, poetry provides us with a means of understanding ourselves and others, of providing empathetic engagement.

4 Padel, Ruth. *The Poem and the Journey:60 Poems for the Journey of Life.* Vintage, London, 2008, 51.

This anthology, *This Gift, This Poem* is the brainchild of Associate Professor Carolyn Rickett from Avondale University who has done much work with people suffering from illness. It is intended to be a book of comfort, joy, revelation, hope and connection. The poems are all contemporary poems written by Australians. Over the past decades Australian poetry has developed into one of the most engaging in the English-speaking world. These poems, while portraying a universal set of emotions, display the music, speech rhythms and perspectives that are uniquely Australian. We hope you enjoy and derive much pleasure from these poems, these gifts.

Judith Beveridge

soul clap

Magdalena Ball

there's no boat
the island, no country

roads peter to glade
glade to open vista
if the day is clear

the artist colony
your corporate body
remains in perpetual youth

gathering loose cells
words like insects
bound in time's honey

perceptions past
passing, or to come
cohere

bind, cling, fuse
grow
into song

the golden bough
your woods
this is the gift

from one microorganism
breathing out carbon
otherwise scattered, lost

to be found here
in this space whole
pulled in, collected
and shared

Reflection

'soul clap', the title of which comes from a line in W B Yeats'
'Sailing to Byzantium' ('Soul clap its hands and sing, and louder
sing'), was originally written as a birthday gift for someone. The
poem explores the value of connection, of coming together, and
of finding meaning in that connection. This past year has been a
particularly challenging one for many people, and I've felt such
a strong sense, even hunger, for connectedness communities
supporting one another. We live in a world where the future can
no longer be predicted, but one thing that is certain is that we
will have to take better care of one another. The poem is a small
celebration of community and the way it provides solace against
the changes and challenges of our lives.

Magdalena Ball

To a Garland Maker

Judith Beveridge

It must be good to be a garland-maker—
your daughters carrying water, working with you
braiding feathers, shells, leaves, repeating the holy names
as they wreathe their fingers around the stems.

Daughters who never let the flowers fall to earth,
or bruise the petals. Daughters festooning doorways,
garnishing gateways, prinking up the palisades.
Daughters whose absolute bliss is marrying

themselves to this—baskets at their hips,
plucking flowers, licking threads. Daughters
who will adorn you at your funeral with blossoms
picked at dawn. It must be fine to be

a garland-maker—your daughters working
with you, weaving prayers around leaves, peduncles;
their breath as fresh as jasmine, meadow grass,
sprays of lavender on an evening breeze.

Reflection

Like all art, poetry has varying approaches: it can be dramatic, narrative, epic, epigrammatic, surreal, irrational, it can highlight the structures and forms within language itself, but it is perhaps the lyric, with its unique characteristics of brevity, musicality, concentration of thought and emotion in a formalised way, which best exemplifies a poem's ability to reverberate and animate consciousness, to bring us into connection with the inner life. I have chosen 'To a Garland Maker' because I am drawn towards poems of praise, those poems which remind us of the wonder of existence. It is my hope that the poem's music and repeating structures will give pleasure to the reader and enact and embody the binding relationships of a shared profession. We know that repeated structures have a calming and stilling effect, as in mantra repetition, often allowing the excess noise of the mind to drop away and to help create deep stillness. The American poet Edward Hirsch has said that 'repetitions loosen the intellect for reverie.' I hope my poem will remind readers that poetry emerged out of song, chanting and dance, those universal human acts of ritual and prayer that attempt to speak of the sacred mystery of experience.

Judith Beveridge

Dancing time and space

Jenny Blackford

I

Men are not forbidden here,
but seldom risk this hall
packed full with women of a certain age.

– Mindful attention to the knees.

Poor Emma Bovary was just a needy child,
sad Anna K not thirty
when they died so painfully.

– Eyes softly focussed.

It's safe to say that most of us
are twice their age or more, well past
hope or fear of tragic passion.

– Mindful attention to the hips.

We do our best to undulate our stiffened bones
like yogic cats, like swaying trees,
like steadfast Sanskrit-speaking warriors.

– Soft face, easy breath.

We are an antique navy of creaking ships
afloat on the parquet floor
in boat pose, the *navasana*.

— Mindful attention to the back.

We pull our navels gently to our spines,
breathe in, breathe out,
breathe in.

— Slow breath, steady mind.

We breathe.

II

Standing, we are Shiva, dancing time
and space into being, perhaps a little wobbly
over rusty ankles on our rainbow mats.

Still, poised with one knee just-bent,
braced, strong, the other hip swung open
like the gate to a new multiverse,

its thigh and foot high-tilted, balanced
by ballerina hands held sideways-lifted
in a frozen moment from creation's dance,

we touch the electricity
of space and time.

Reflection

Almost every week for the last ten years, I've gone to the same yoga class, run by the same patient and careful teacher, in the same draughty parquet-floored hall, with mostly the same people, mostly women, and most of us definitely of a certain age. Every time, the teacher guides us through variations on exercises and asanas, all carefully structured to ensure that the right parts of our bodies are stretched or strengthened, and that our minds are calmed.

I doubt that I'm getting any better at it. I still wobble during all the balances, and there are some poses where I've learned to take the easier option offered by our teacher. All the same, it takes a lot to keep me away from this gentle yet demanding exercise. Just being there, doing it, as part of the group, can be sublime.

Jenny Blackford

Paralysis

Peter Boyle

Laid out flat
in the back of the station wagon my father borrowed
I look up:
the leaves are immense,
green and golden with clear summer light
breaking through –
though I turn only my neck
I can see all of them
along this avenue that has no limits.

What does it matter
that I am only eyes
if I am to be carried
so lightly
under the trees of the world?
From beyond the numbness of my strange body
the wealth of the leaves
falls forever
into my small still watching.

Reflection

Shortly before my third birthday I contracted poliomyelitis, as did many children in Australia in the early 1950s before the vaccine was invented. From my navel down my body was paralysed. I could move my arms and neck but not sit up by myself or walk. Over time mobility came back to all my limbs apart from my right leg.

I don't remember the long stay in an isolation ward or much of the subsequent months. My first memory in life is of lying in the back of a station wagon my father had borrowed from a friend to move us from one house to another in Melbourne. I remember the journey up an avenue of trees and, afterwards, I remember my father carrying me around the garden of the new house.

This poem which contains my first memory in life feels particularly special to me. I read it at my father's funeral. I can see it now from two sides. From the point of view of the child, the one suffering or disabled, there is the immense richness of the earth's protection and of parental love. Even when life is reduced to the minimum there is this potential for sensing and gathering in the wonder of what lies around us, a sense of being not blighted but blessed. I can also see the poem from the point of view of the parents who doubtless felt completely devastated seeing their child lying there helpless. As a parent with my own children I can feel the sorrow and pain they must have felt, unable to know the calm joy that was in that small child as he let himself be transported from house to house under the sheltering trees. I hadn't really thought much of this memory until I wrote the poem in my late forties. It is in the present tense because deep things are in the present tense, settling into our sense of who we are.

I believe there is in the smallest things of life—sunlight, the trees, the sea or a river glimpsed as we pass by—an immense wealth that can pour into us when we need it. There is a mystery within suffering so that, at least in certain moments, it is not all suffering.

Peter Boyle

The Shower Stall

Lisa Brockwell

Wisdom does not follow conquest,
although I tend to fall into thinking so.
Sitting here, on a milk crate,
watching the easy bounty
of bore water sluice over her leg,
holding the hose high above her knee,
so the current cascades down slender cannon
to film and bulb the swell of fetlock
and then rush away over coronet, hoof,
concrete floor, to pool among blue top,
farmer's friend, toads, dragonfruit rot,
wild raspberry bushes that house
the black, spare fairy-wrens
with their flash of slapstick orange.

A slow sulphur of pain,
low and new in my back, I rest
my forehead against her belly, listen
to the secret world of digestion
and the ever-present electrics
of a prey animal, tranquillized for now
by the water whispering to her hot leg,
by my hand on her shoulder,
but ever alert below the surface,
like a bream ready to dart
for insects that sit and skim.

The infection is no worse,
nothing rising but the grass
grown too long,

once the rains have stopped
the tractor will come to slash
the paddocks, until then,
the weeds have won.

Ants retreat down a fencepost;
flushing the black pepper
of grass seed out of the wound,
I feel a shift in pressure
under the iron hull of cloud
before the next deluge. A magpie
calls bright and clear in the lull,
teaching its juvenile to hunt,
to be, and a large butterfly
appears, solitary, wings the dark
grain of cedar or mahogany.

The world ripples when I stand,
unwell, I guess, but not enough
to notice until I'm in the realm
of the physical: paddocks, mud,
boots, wheelie bin of chaff
smelling sweeter than the cakes
never baked in my childhood oven.

Autumn is around the corner
with its mornings of mist and promise
of dry days. The rain, now,
when it comes, is cooler
than I expect. It runs down
my back in rivulets, soothes
the burr of fever against my skin.
I can no longer see the hills, all
is valley now, all closed in. The young
magpie dips and jogs, staccato,

across the round ring,
looking for the worm.

Reflection

I find it difficult to say anything at all sensible about the poems
I've written, and would consider myself one of the people least
qualified to do so. Writing a poem is a mysterious process and a
poem becomes itself by and through the very act of being made. I
don't think a poem is *about* something, rather it becomes something
through being composed, and then being read by someone else.
A poem charts and maps the human process of thinking in
language, circling back, trying out phrases, struggling to construct
some kind of meaning in the world, and this poem was written
during a time of my life just before a profound transformation:
the end of a long marriage, my son reaching adolescence and the
subsequent change in my role as his mother, the beginning of a
new relationship, my decision to move from Australia to Scotland.
None of this had happened yet, in the poem I'm nursing my horse
who was seriously injured after getting herself tangled in barbed
wire. Looking back, I can see it might be read as a meditation on
time, healing and vulnerability. At the time all I knew was that I
was feeling stalled, and that I needed to keep taking responsibility
for those I loved and was responsible for.

Lisa Brockwell

Reverse Haibun

Andrew Burke

measuring the step
with her chin —
blind dog.

~

My dog wants an appearance fee
for yesterday's haiku. Okay, I say,
and give her a *Smacko* (Beef).
Not good enough, she wants two.
No way! Think of your weight!
But dogs think in the present tense,
no future worries. To avoid
contractual headaches, I stop
writing about her. She humphs
and goes through her doggy door
to tell the moon her grievances.

Reflection

I have had a dog all my life, starting with Minnie the Moocher when I was a toddler in the 1940s. Then followed Wire-haired terriers, bitzers, dingo pups, long haired Labrador, Jack Russells, a delightful Maltese cross and – perhaps my favourite – Millie, the black Cavoodle. This is my poem to her.

When Millie was older and showing signs of slowing down, I was living in a strange town with my wife but no writing mates and the poetry push I had back in Perth. Millie was my mate. We explored the old township and the small town memorials, cemeteries, school yards and churches. I was a little poorly, so she would come and collect me at 4pm and demand a nap. Every day. I didn't argue.

Millie was a highly intelligent dog – people say this was because she had Poodle in her. But most of all she was my mate when I was lonely.

What sort of poem is it? Well, the Japanese have a wonderful traditional form that is written in short prose then followed by a haiku, called Haibun. I wrote the haiku first, then Millie came up, put her forepaws on me, tongue hanging out, like she expected a reward for being in the poem. It is simply my quirk to reverse the form.

Andrew Burke

Homer Nods

William Christie

'By melancholy, saith [Aristotle], some men are made as it were divine,
foretelling things to come, and some men are made poets'
Cornelius Agrippa,
De Occulta Philosophia

'Tell me, Asklepios, housed on Olympus, you who know
All carnal and all psychic things; whose light can penetrate
the deep caverns of disturbèd mind (for I am humbled, and only
know the humour; am wounded and only know the pain):
Whence this visitation? These sea-dark moods, with sighs
and baleful groans attended? Whither is fled the ease
of sleep, the liquid pleasures of the tongue and loins?
And why are these most noble mountains, lustrous plains,
Why is the rich *poesis* of the protean sea, suddenly
obscured by shadows—without beauty, without love?'
So Homer prayed. In time the prayer itself would lose
its point and purpose, dissolving with the urge to utterance.

Still Calliope shared possession of his mind, whence flowed
exalted songs of gods and heroes; of noble Odysseus above all,
his surpassing cunning and his courage chanted forth.
After betrayal, battle; after tight rage, abundant rhetoric;
after protracted war in Ilion, protracted journey;
after the long-suffering Odysseus, strategist supreme,
contended with both foe and fate—homecoming.
Ithaka is won back, and Odysseus' rich mantle drawn at last.

So fares the tale. Far-famed Odysseus, sailor of deceitful seas,
alive in the congregated mind of Hellas and the West,
sleeps in the fraught imagination of his maker.
                                   So fares the tale,
but not the teller so. And what if Homer nods? What if the bard
is blessed by Hypnos with beseeched repose? 'Tis surely just:
long afternoons—agonies in which the Ionian sunshine forms
a blinding, iridescent robe upon a seething, ageless sea—
weigh in the blood and slow down the heart, seeming
to last forever: the heavy ache of lethargy, without escape.

Reflection

'I writ of melancholy, by being busy to avoid melancholy', wrote
Robert Burton in his famous *Anatomy*. Burton knew well the
susceptibility of poets to self-doubt and depression and in this
poem I take literally the famous eighteenth-century critical
axiom, 'Homer nods' – meaning that even Homer slackens off
and errs on occasion – to refer to Homer's struggle with insomnia
and life-long melancholia. 'For he who much has suffer'd, much
will know', he says in *The Odyssey* (Book 15). This speculative
fantasy, then, written in loose hexameters and using Homer as the
archetypal poet, suggests that out of suffering much can be made,
and much beauty can come.

William Christie

Our mothers, the trees.

Josephine Clarke

In the days of deluge
— *fear, trauma, grief* —
we women
cup our hands through water,
make slow progress
through the oily slough.

We drift, sucked by the tide,
our silks and cashmeres useless,
adornments giving small purchase.

We search a watery horizon,
settle at the trees,
on old growth.

Wood we feel
with our fingers,
our palms;
time and our hands reciting
the lines of wisdom.

Old wood.
All our mothers.
Our mothers' mothers;
icons in silver,
years of living ingrained,
scars worn to gleam.

Our gaze is locked
towards such constancy,
such strength in storms.

Reflection

Who can explain the consolation of wood? We bend over to pick
up a piece of driftwood and our fingers trace the worn shape, feel
the softness of its brined state. There is something about it that we
want to hold on to.

We stand at the base of an old tree and join hands with our children
to measure its girth. Our heads bend back to look up and see the
sky beyond its reach. We lean into the years of slow growth and
imagine the many weathers the tree has withstood: sheeting rain,
threshing winds, desiccating summers. Being in the forest is deeply
replenishing for me. I love watching rain run down tree trunks,
see eucalypts shed an old bark to reveal a new sheen. In summer
you can hear karri trees drying, branches creaking and cracking as
their water load recedes. It reminds me of life's rhythm; its endless
push forward.

There is so much that is beautiful about aging. So often we are
comforted by being near those who have known more of life.
I wrote this poem shortly after my mother died. It describes
something of what I missed about having elders close by.

Josephine Clarke

Pilgrim

Kerryn Coombs-Valeontis

every 20 – 60 years
when it is told
that the flowers are returned
like persephone or odysseus,
meet me in the violet-blue
mountain uplift
warping and faulting
ascend with me the high passes and let us
traverse out onto triassic basalt
and claystone plateau,
let our lungs, still tight
with the memory of smoke
breathe in mountains, busy
healing themselves, take my hand
where the waratah's
striving back in charcoaled monocline
of stump-blackened gums
in the absence of birdsong
let it be late
when quartzose fluvial
sandstone stretches on tip-toe
for last embrace
of warmth, take off your shoes
tread softly, pink-brushed flannel petals
like stars at our feet, behold
the triumph of drought-fire-rain
sequence, that is all this land knows;
tarry with me,
til stratus-thin fuchsia-whisp glaze
the evening, and we

have filled our heart-bags with rosy stars
descend with me to the world overlaid
with carpets of them – a world
all flower-smitten

Reflection

This poem came from a trip up the Blue Mountains to see the
pink flannel flowers, a phenomenon only usually seen once in
a lifetime. These uniquely Australian flowers only come after
extreme fires, following the rain that inevitably, eventually arrives.
The flowers were very crowded, as many people wanted to make
the pilgrimage up there – a collective healing invitation, after the
bushfires of 2019/2020 and their devastation. We were there on
evening, to avoid the crowds, when the sky reflected the unique
colouring of these rare and breathtaking mass bloomings. The
flannel flower has been chosen to symbolise adaptability, resilience
and endurance, for good mental health. The poem was further
inspired, by viewing Dharug artist Dianne Ussher's commissioned
artwork celebrating the resilience and healing journey, of her
people, called 'The medicine woman of the flannel flower.' It can
be viewed at https://ice.org.au/2021/01/medicine-women-of-the-flannel-
flower-dianne-ussher/

Kerryn Coombs-Valeontis

Trees that Speak and Dream

Judith Nangala Crispin

I am beginning to see as the dog sees, this desert light quickening to sunfire. Mirage makes the sky edgeless. Over Indangangu salt lake, a Nankeen Kestrel drops in blueness, like a seed.

We camp under warding trees – *Wapurnungku*, Ghost Gum, *Wirrka-li*, Bloodwood, *Kurrkara*, Desert Oak – rooted in the swales between wind-sculpted dunes, where sand falls deep and red.

We're so far out now … so far from houses or roads. Behind us, the Wailbri Ranges are a faint band, studded with lights from uranium mines.

No one stops here for long without a campfire, not even in daylight. Fire keeps predators away, dingoes and snakes, shadows that move independently of the sun.

Cowled in smoke, the dog rotates an ear toward the west where a low wind drones around Mount Wedge and down into *Palka-Karrinya*, bringing offerings of burned leaves to the owl-shaped stone in the valley mouth.

When mind is quiet like this, when it's still, you can hear the desert singing – finches landing in grevillea, water slides over striated rock. Under a rock pool's lip, two snakes breathe in long heavy sighs.

But here, by this salt lake, trees turn their fingers in the light. Their weightless reaches vanish in leafshine. In the old language, a single word exists for branches and wings.*

The Nankeen Kestrel circles, lands in heartwood, merges with the oak's furrowed skin.

Its barred tail camouflaged against the snake-vine winding like dreadlocks down the trunk. And beneath this sand, taproots push through rocks and loam, into the water table.

Some nights, if you lie with your stomach to the earth, you can sense the intelligence of this desert falling through those loose roots. And we are rooted in them, the dog and me, this smoking branch, they carry us.

When it's windless, when the sands are moonlit and smooth, you can hear trees speaking in their slow electric language, their bark growling, sap pumping like blood.

Sometimes we've woken, in our terrible separateness, to find a tree's wing spread above us. Fanned out between us and the sky. And we've known, if we'd not moved then, we might've grown into the ground.

From this place you can turn a circle and see the curvature of the earth – scattered planets, the firefly stars. In the Pleaides, cosmic trees sow their seeds in space. Corona Australis is a crescent of ghost gums. Their branches host clouds of interstellar grasshoppers. Vela's neutron star, rotating 11 times a second, creates their song.

The dog and I are curling to sleep, our swag softened by smoke, in the steady breathing of the oaks, the humming stars, the whole landscape listening.

(* Kilpirli)

Reflection

During COVID we were all cut off from the humans that we love. It's easy to feel very alone in lockdown. But our community is much greater than the human world. We live in the company of great trees, in the embrace of wise dogs, with the tolerance of cats. It is only our enculturation that claims it's possible to be alone in a forest or a desert, alone in a house, alone in a street. And maybe, if we could see a pot-plant or a goldfish as a being, in every way as sentient and miraculous as a human being, we'd realise that we're never alone. Perhaps part of human resilience is to do with this — with being part of an extraordinary symbiotic ecosystem, not just an individual. All over the world, during these days of plague, people have uploaded photos and descriptions of trees. Trees outside apartment windows or seen from hospitals. Imagined or remembered trees. I've written this poem to share my own experience of the intelligence of trees — the intelligence of some of the most remote trees in this country, in the central desert.

Judith Nangala Crispin

'The sparrow sits ...'

MTC Cronin

The sparrow sits
like a stranger on your sill.
Stars don't work on you
like they used to.
You need a song that's closer.
With wild grace
the bird takes the crumb
from your hand.
But it is your hand that begged.

Reflection

The only epiphany is one that has no need to occur.

MTC Cronin

Cranes fly on my blue and white porcelain brooch

Jan Dean

Kiyomizu Temple Precinct, Kyoto

People take several paths and transformations
to find and leave a closer view of the summit.
Some wait until mid-morning. Others

depart with pilgrims and lose themselves
in the mists of dawn. None may go further

than halfway. The summit is simply a frame
        for platforms that cling to the slope.
I began at the launch pad and proceeded on foot

up the river of light, reminiscent of a ramp
        on the face of a Mayan temple.

Close to the entrance souvenir shops
crowd the road into an avenue, confetti-bright.
Kindly avoid temptation until the return journey.

A few, as feathers floated by a gentle breeze
take the thin path on the left hand side facing the city.

        In which case, they choose the time
of ancestor reverence, when final resting spots
marked by tall stones of charcoal flecked with white

diffused over the vast curve, enjoy blessings;
single red roses, mingling with companions

to set the sweep ablaze.
The right path is narrow and steep enough
to persuade a caterpillar persona. It is pleasurable

however inclement the weather. Rain,
may increase your chances of being charmed

by sheen on cobblestones, heel-clack & feet-shuffle
or navy & white *noren*, damp yet aflutter
        and the women

who surge into doorways and turn to face you
as parasols collapse into narrow vees

under facades; compact, mature, ghostly.
Back on level ground, you should meander over
to Gion in time for twilight, when lit paper lanterns

proclaim trainee geishas, who perfect their art
of fragility hovering on platform shoes.

Ruby lips and mime-like faces emit no emotion
yet receive the respect reserved for dolls
preserved in museums. They pose then disappear

silk kimonos rustling rainbows, and somewhere
        along the way, I found my prize.

Note: A noren is a 'doorway curtain' hanging in front of a shop to announce the specialty within.

Reflection

'Cranes fly on my blue and white porcelain brooch' reminds of a special time in my life just prior to retirement when I spent six months in Japan as an exchange teacher of English. I was stationed at Tanagura, Fukushima in 1995 and halfway through the duration travelled with my husband by bullet train to Kyoto where the area around the Buddhist Kiyomizu Temple Precinct made a powerful impression for its splendour, unique and long-lasting traditions and religious significance. I bought the brooch as a memento. Touching the simple porcelain rectangle, smooth with three raised cranes in flight, revives feelings of that wonderful occasion. In Asia, cranes symbolise vigilance, purity, longevity and harmony between wealth (not necessarily financial) and faith. I hope my poem concerning the brooch and its connections invokes for readers the calm, joy and thrill of discovery we experienced.

Jan Dean

Netball in Newlyn

Ross Donlon

For my daughter, Eithne

Newlyn is quiet,
only shadows play in the park.
Then netball lights flicker,
kick on. Drills start
as stars connect
above the turquoise court,
tiny, turquoise planet,
gold rings at each end.
Light bulbs grow worlds
freckled with moths.
Girls run and shout,
arms outstretched.
Sneakers squeak.
A mum calls out instructions.
And I'm glad there's netball in Newlyn,
a blink-and-you-missed-it place
whose lights dissolve as you climb the hill.
It gives me heart to see them train,
to run and pass almost by instinct.
It reminds me how we make and do
in Newlyn, or New York, or anywhere
someone tries to do something
more than survive a night and day.
It's why I write – to move space, imagine,
make order of emotion, thought, action,
try to score a goal.

Reflection

The poem tells its own story. I was driving though Newlyn, a hamlet between Ballarat and Daylesford, one evening at dusk where netball practice had started. It made me think of human habitation all over the world, big cities and villages, those tiny lights you see from 30,000 feet, where people are continuing to make and play with the unconscious desire to go on. It's a tremendous power, the drive or will to go on, to get better if we're ill, and to use the time we have to make and do the best we can, or simply to have fun.

Ross Donlon

Night List

Lucy Dougan

I sleep with a cat and a man.
I sleep with the man every night.
The cat I share with a neighbour.
I sleep beneath the Navaho patterned knee rug
a daughter left behind
and also when it is cold, her brown cardigan.
I sleep in socks a little too large,
blue, marl, again left behind, this time by a son
who told me the other day he had found peace.
I am building this armour in my bed
of the man, the cat, the rug, the socks
that wards off how I begin to feel when the air gets dark.
Beneath the armour is my body, of course,
which has not always been the most reliable of bodies.
But I begin to invent a companion anatomy of goods
that abide in its dark cavity,
eggs hiding maybe even still.
Are they, I read somewhere,
eggs that were in your grandmother and right back beyond?
And also another thing I read,
in it are housed remnants of the children I have had:
boy, boy, girl—I do hope that is so—
my own boy, boy, girl, man, cat,
rug, cardigan, socks, eggs, remnants
of those carried and born.
Rain outside now making its own patient list.
We're all accounted for here and good.

Reflection

I've been thinking about armour a lot. I have thought especially about the amazing scene in Pedro Almodóvar's film *Talk to Her* in which the matador character Lydia is helped into her *traje de luces*. I find the intersections of vulnerability, strength and ritual in that scene very moving. So, I want to offer this poem to any reader who might be in need of some homemade armour. I hope that my poem shows that it can be built out of the simplest things to hand: things you carry within you and things that may come to you by serendipity. And also, that building it can become part of the rhythm of your day or night. I hope, too, there comes a time when you can shed your armour, but always know that it's possible to shed and rebuild it as often as necessary.

Lucy Dougan

Ribbons

Ali Cobby Eckerman

'See you' I said to the children
as I memorised
their Anangu faces
filled with laughter
and trust for family
innocent in their youth
and strong in culture

'See you' I said to the Elders
as the tears flow
in my heart
and I bend down
to shake their hands
and gain my strength
by skin

'See you' I said at Murputja
and the dust from my car
as I drove away
was like a ribbon
across the desert sand
tying me to that place
forever

Reflection

For most people life travels us. Often we are removed from the place we love the most, due to employment or marriage or opportunity. The impact of these sacrifices differs for each of us. The benefits can vary too. This is the nature of modern life.

Often the yearning for home is kept deep within us. As humans we have learned to adapt to changes, rewarded by new securities and success. However, the primal yearning encourages us to revisit the places we love at every possible occasion.

The desert is the place I love best. This is the landscape in which my soul feels most secure. I carry each treasured moment within me. And when I return every memory blooms inside. The essence of this blossoming holds the power to heal me. It is important to honour both our inherited and personal stories. A special gift of living.

Ali Cobby Eckerman

Here and Now

Stephen Edgar

A rustle in the leaves. One lorikeet
Emerges on a bending stem
To dangle,
While feeding upside down among the sweet
Grevillea flowers at a reckless angle.

In real time, the shadows under them
Make copies on the courtyard bricks.
A skink
Lies practising its brilliant stratagem,
To stare into the sun and not to blink,

A miniature bronze sculpture, till it licks
An errant ant with perfect aim.
The sky,
Drying in blue enamel, tries to affix
One cloud in place before it passes by.

A curtain cord taps on the window frame
Arrhythmically in a faint breeze,
As though
Too quick to hit the beat, making the same
Mistake a few times, then, instead, too slow.

A sort of dreamlike present tense—which frees
The mind from the entanglements
Of nerve
And muscle, all those hinged complexities
We're made of, with their claims on those they serve—

A sort of disembodied present tense
Pervades this setting to suspend
The day,
As though you were what you experience,
Part of the elements through which you stray,

Persuading you that this will never end.

Reflection

One of the epigraphs that Patrick White chose for his novel *The Solid Mandala* is by Paul Eluard: 'There is another world, but it is in this one.' I have always been drawn to the quotation, partly, it seems to me, because it encapsulates something that I try to evoke from time to time in my own poetry, and 'Here and Now' is one example. I am not speaking about epiphany, not at least if that word is taken to refer to some revelation of the supernatural or divine, but rather a mental state in which focus on the natural surroundings causes the ego, the self, to go briefly into abeyance. You escape the prison of the mind and seem to become absorbed into some more primal state, however transiently. This can be quietly exhilarating.

I don't think that it is an intrinsic purpose of poetry to provide solace, although that is not to say that people may not sometimes draw solace from it. Rather, in my case, it is an attempt to recreate in the reader a striking and memorable experience, whatever its character, in a form of words which is equally striking and memorable.

Stephen Edgar

Sun-shower

Theodore Ell

Late in the year, a lifted blind

let in reunions. Light beating on the leaves.
A likeness had come over the days

to forerunners peopled with smaller shadows,

as though old friends were coming home
to bargain for extensions on the past,

make disclosures from before
the crowding-out of life. Hesitant warmth

in light of words that left their handprints on the mirror.

Pressure to tread lightly
on the grass spears, barefoot even:

there was recovery in the turf
though a sole could best what the drought had not.

Then the clouds, encountering errors, thinned away.

Not the peace we were preparing for –
though perhaps a truce with silence.

A noon for me, a keepsake.

Reflection

For some years, particularly in my twenties, I made my most meaningful connections with people from whom I would soon be separated by a great distance. They might move to another city or overseas or remain in a faraway place while I returned home, or perhaps they would be consumed with work or obligations, where I had little or few.

Some of these connections endured. They are friendships that thrive even in absence. The first moments of a conversation can bridge years.

Other friendships live only in memory. It is hard to say when, or why, in such long periods without a word, the instinct to make contact waned. I think back and back.

Today, as distance forces itself between us with new harshness, it is heartening to recover even the faintest trace of these bonds, revived by some chance event. What seemed to slip to the edges of life is held still in the mind.

When you read this poem, I hope you may catch a glimpse, in your mind's eye, of the people of your past who still affect you and whose company is still as real as when you first experienced it.

Theodore Ell

Lingering

Robert Edmonds

There's a child in paediatric intensive care
and I dare not meet his eyes

My first ever day of paid work
I'm in a coal washery
wondering if I should have worn longer socks to keep my legs warm
when my boss is stung by a wasp
Bugger it, he says, flicks it off his arm and keeps on working

I'm talking to a sixteen year old man
with an intellectual disability
whose parents beat him, whose girlfriend is pregnant, who's doing his HSC
I don't cut anymore, he says
Look
I took your advice
I catch and release venomous snakes
He's beaming now
and in every picture on his phone

My dad, at 90, every few months
to fight off the fog of macular degeneration
sits patiently looking at the wall
while a doctor puts a needle into each of his eyes
That generation, they're a race apart, says the doctor

And I am a clown and I have entered a room
where a boy is on some kind of respirator
and Everything Ridiculous has finally caught up
and entered with me
When our eyes meet, before I even speak, his eyes wrinkle up

and he starts to laugh and as he laughs, he chokes
I back away
Come back, he says
I come back to the door
He cracks up
and starts to suffocate
I back away
and there, in the corridor
I linger
Come back, he says
We always push
at boundaries
You can tell us to be careful
but what people do
is push
Eventually
all of us will push and keep pushing
And I am lingering in this corridor
boy
ready for you

Reflection

I've chosen this poem because it's partly set in hospital. It's about how people push at boundaries. Sometimes they push because they are resilient and sometimes they push boundaries in completely unexpected ways. I've learnt that people (even young people) are unique and complicated. And they get more complicated as they get older.

When people get a whiff of hope they push even harder. I don't know where hope comes from, but it comes running when it hears the sound of laughter. When people are low and flat emotionally, they can't see very far. But lift their spirits and you lift their perspective too.

Humour is a great way to lift spirits. It's like a lightning rod for hope. And it is powerful. It's also subversive and unpredictable and surprising, just like creativity.

All of things in this poem really happened. They shocked me. And then they made me wonder.
I'd love it if this poem went some small way toward doing the same for you.

Robert Edmonds

Rain as it is

Brook Emery

Rain as it is only brighter. Momentarily the luminous is
    threading through the grey. So tempting to affirm:

the commonplace is beautiful and still surprising. Now
    glistening shades of green, the pure white

crumpled flowers, there the purple I thought black, and deeper
    all the hidden, tangled world: might unbearable be that
    which must be borne,

what can't be shed or shucked? Nearby a voice says, with all my
    heart; someone else can't speak at all; and the rain keeps
    coming down.

Almost everything can be explained. We forget, choose not to
    think, or in the moment

surrender to an incessant we know will pass, mystery with as
    many forms as birds have different wings.

Dear K, this particular rain is here at last and we are wet and
    alive and laughing

that in all this pitiless world what touches us now with its
    unbidden grace, its dripping material thingitude, is just
    this rain.

Reflection

'Rain as it is' is the last poem in my book *Collusion* (JLP, 2012). It is meant as a bookend to the first poem which is also addressed to an unidentified 'K' who may be a real correspondent, may be the self, or may be the unconscious. It is a conclusion to the loose argument of the book which puzzles about the intersections between the material, the spiritual and the rational. I think the poem affirms that, despite doubts and difficulties and pain, it is possible to find beauty and joy and solace, at least momentarily, in the physical and natural if only we give ourselves up to the experience. It is important to me that the rain is as real as it is ambiguously symbolic.

Brook Emery

On the Organic Form of Art

Luke Fischer

There are those who question
your talk of organic form,
regard it a mere hypothesis
or wishful thinking, as though you were
proposing poetry as a solution to climate change,
the road to renewable energies. And you
are, obliquely, but that aside, you remember
the concert where within the air, the reverse
side of space, the vast rooms that open
behind the closed curtains of your eyes,
rhythms and melodies became pulsing images,
expanding and contracting forms
like breath or tides, buds and
blossoms, a circle dance of figures
joining, releasing hands, yourself among them ...
and the depression you had carried with you
into the hall—the depression of our times
whether diagnosed or not—lifted
unnoticed as dew that bends
grassblades before the dawn. Integrated
in this cosmophony, you left the auditorium
with a lighter gait, the subtle smile of a kouros
on your lips. The street's architecture, the aureole
of lamps—extending the twilight of evening
into night—the fluid lines of *Jugendstil*
seemed the setting of a tale.

But returning to your argument,
the other side of air: Who were
these mobile creatures lining space?

Of music that wouldn't sound without
human endeavour? Human creatures, then,
and yet more than human, what once
were considered daimonic
inventions, dictations of a demi-god:
true as lizards, koalas, cicadas, eucalypts,
similarly unique in their dynamic ratios—
tempo, time and rhythm, their heartbeat and breath,
melodic phrases, their expressive action—
so many variations on the one
theme. Though they lived
only as long as the music endured
their harmony reverberated in your sleep
and the strange serenity in which
you woke the next day.

Why share this now?
Outcast from the Self, exiled
from the cosmos, a shadow abiding
in a world conquered by Hades,
in memory you locate the cave-mouth,
the entry to the upper world, this poem
a longing for organic form ...

Reflection

I chose to contribute 'On the Organic Form of Art' to this anthology as it explores the power of art, music and poetry to transport us, to lift us into a realm that transcends our daily concerns. Although the speaker in the poem feels alienated from this higher dimension of art, this dimension can be glimpsed again by way of recollection. During difficult times we can find solace in joyful memories, which, for me, include those moments in which I have been struck by the beauty and expansiveness of a singular piece of music, painting or poem. This sense of transcendence is not an escape from the earth to an otherworldly sphere, rather it conveys a deepened feeling of connection to the whole of existence. The notion that artworks have an organic form—that they embody the holistic integrity of a living organism—has been elaborated by various romantic and modern thinkers. I particularly like Johann Wolfgang von Goethe's characterisation of art as the 'spiritual-organic' because it pithily suggests that art can lift us into the spiritual realm while at the same time revealing the cohesive unity of diverse forms of nature.

Luke Fischer

Dancing with Stephen Hawking

John Foulcher

for Melinda Smith

I was living in England. Punk days, they were.
On my way to the party, I fell and scraped skin
from my knees, tore my stockings. No matter,
they were punk days, and I looked the part —
black-root blonde, make-up slurring my face.
And there she was: *He wants to dance with you.*
And there he was, seeping into his chair, mind
in the machine. From a distance, I'd thought him
all thought, the body's ruin savaging desire,
but something simmered there. He rolled across
the wooden floor like a ship leaving harbour,
adrift on a wide sea. I did my best punk moves,
spasmodic thrusts and jumps, while he swayed
left then right in his choreography of wheels.
I tried not to stare. We moved until the music
slammed into silence, left everyone talking
too loud for a moment, like the noise of insects
in the dark. I don't recall talking at all, only
the time given ... Walking to the station,
I stopped, looked up to a moonless sky,
wondering whether that cloud was a cloud
or a galaxy. And I thought of the dance
of asteroids, the merciless pull of black holes,
red giants and white dwarves, breathless
nebulae. I thought of the atoms in my eye,
spinning and spinning, and the torrent of light
surging through me, soaking me to the bone
as I stood looking up, with my bloodied knees.

Reflection

'Dancing with Stephen Hawking' is based on the experience of my colleague, Melinda Smith. It was written with her permission and approval. I've always admired Stephen Hawking, but like the narrator of this poem, I'd always assumed him 'all thought'. Melinda's experience, though, hints otherwise — despite his severe disabilities, it seems Hawking was not only a man of vivid and imaginative intellect, but he also felt the pleasures of the physical world. It suggested to me that we are all both hindered and enriched by the body's limitations, that we can all reach for the stars, as they say, no matter how bloodied our knees are.

John Foulcher

Toddler with Neptune's Necklace

Kathryn Fry

She bends to waft her fingers in the rock pool,
and lingers there, as if she's listening
to a lullaby before sleep. I break off

a strand, her eyes follow its thin float.
She picks it up, squeezes a bead
then another, thumb and first finger

on the firm baubles. She turns them,
till she spots how light is caught like honey
beyond the dark marks of the skin.

I point to limpets stuck like cone-hats
and the zebra snail at the end of its track,
sand piled on the sides of its narrow winding

path. She eyes other crop on the rock
and now, when I hoist her up onto the ledge,
she discovers how to glide over

the lumpy cover of necklaces and slip
down into the water; the chill rising to her chest.
I point to the fleeting shadows of small fish

but she wants the ledge, to toe-grip the algae
before she drops; we do this again and again,
and each time her shrieks spell a new thrill.

Reflection

I was with our youngest granddaughter the first time she visited a rock pool at Merewether Beach. She was nearly two years old and I was keen to show her the animals and algae. However, I was surprised when she discovered her own game there, even though the water was quite cool. And perhaps even more surprising was how she shrieked with excitement when she slid down the algae from the ledge, as if each time was the first. And then I remembered that's how we learn, by doing something repeatedly. Her sheer delight in being engaged with life and learning was obvious. I hope this poem brings you some of the joy and exuberance in a child's life – especially with being in a natural setting. Maybe it'll even take you there so you'll 'hear' the sounds of the sea beyond.

Kathryn Fry

For my daughters, Gemma and Amber

Althea Halliday

This year I am stitching my words into stories —
the ones about my childhood
that I told you in your childhood,
and the ones of our own making.

There will be others, of course —
the awkwardness of growing up tall,
the school principal who pointed me past Year 10 to teaching,
Julius Caesar and the rabble that almost drove me out of Rome,
your father in Melbourne, Fangio in his new Toyota,
loving me then,
and loving us now.

The words will be worked on the finest fabric.
I will use threads that I know you will recognise,
and yarns that were made well before your time.
Woven as one, they will remind us of who we are
and the roads that have been taken.

The tales of the bush will be done in green and brown.

There will be images of spotted gums and wattle, bee-heavy with flowers,
ducks in full sail on the dam,
the big bay mare in grass up to her girth.

The brown will be for the droughts.

The colours of the gullies and the sea and the sky
will thread your journeys through childhood.
You will see the rock pools and the maiden hair fern,

the canvas of sand and the shells that you curled in your hands.

I will chain stitch these to our journeys abroad.
Your father, as always, will be at the wheel –
memorising spirax maps in the campervan,
reversing the hire car in breath-stopping narrowness and rain,
easing us impossibly in the people mover through tourists and tables,
pigeons and prams.

And the laughter –
I will make large looping stitches for the laughter:
the Budapest baths, the park in Monza, the stockings in Sicily.

Around the edge of all of this I will embroider a tribute to my mother,
whose toil and love and delight in words nurtured my own words
and sent me soaring past tertiary education and Shakespeare's riot
to students who listened with their heart to the nightingale in Keats
and the angels who sang Hamlet to his rest.

Many of them travelled with me
down the long, splendid corridors of time and space
in *Cloudstreet*.

So, when my stitching is done,
when the yarns are in place and the weaving complete,
I will give each of you this gift.

One for you.

And one for you.

With love.

Reflection

In my early years, our family lived on an isolated cattle property where perseverance in the face of hardship and seasonal uncertainty framed the narratives of our lives. The episodes that became our favourite stories embodied singular courage, stubbornness, eccentricity and humour. My poem reflects the significance of those childhood stories as well as the ones that were made with my husband and our children. It also speaks of the delight that can be found in words – the sheer joy of shaping and sharing our own words, and the words that have been crafted by others. Importantly, it suggests that stories that are retold, in oral form or in writing, are a gift.

In light of a poem being a gift, I offer my words in the hope that in times when our hearts hurt in anxiety and longing, we may find comfort in remembering our best stories: the ones that remind us of so much that we have shared. Through the years, this has been a gift that we have given each other. Perhaps – even in spite of uncertainty and sadness – it can be our gift again.

Althea Halliday

Spring, Oxfam Brochure and Other Gifts

Jennifer Harrison

Spring arrives *a fortiori* and you wake to wattlebirds
your dog's morning greeting, his tail's flutter of happiness.

Sudden rain falls like pebbles rolling in an ocean drum
and the sagging curtains are as frayed as your Papuan billum.

Once, you were given a spiral sculpture of faces
carved from a mango tree and you remember how the eyes

stared forever across opposite deserts or seas.
In the brochure on the table, the capiz-shell

mobiles glitter from the page and outside the window
the jacaranda's new bronze fronds push towards the sun

shadowing out the roughly-planted fennel.
A quiet morning of no special pearliness. Your voice

less gravelly than when you were smoking. Gypsy swing
on the radio. The bed linen coffee-stained.

To think that the Black Princes are unwrapping from their shells
their cicada effigies preparing to crouch like skeleton trolls

on the trellis and ferns—but only after an evening of song.
Doesn't tenderness burn some days

like the last of winter's coals? *A fortiori*. For the bold.

Reflection

I've always liked this poem for its attempt to honour the small moments of happiness, the miniscule delight of encountering wonder in the world – how it can strike so suddenly and randomly, sometimes in the midst of angst or turmoil. How transitory it is. The images are exceptionally ordinary, and rather true. The poem is built around the Latin adverb *a fortiori*, translated here as 'for a still stronger reason; even more certain; all the more'.

Jennifer Harrison

Yet

Dennis Haskell

for Annamaria

I wake beside a hunk of concrete
angled up to a frenzied freeway
where platoons of scooters, trucks
and cars roar insatiably all night long

but they particularly steal my ears
this morning of Christmas Eve.
In Gaoxiong's soupy skies
at night the moon is only visible

occasionally, but I know it's there;
moonbeams, moonshine, *clair de lune*:
all its meanings sound corny
and are given by us, but then

can be reflected back, just as
science says its light is reflection,
mere reflection. In America
a man rants in a department store

'Stop lying to your kids!'
'There is no Santa Claus!'
yet the kids queuing for Santa
ignore his voice. He can't tell

how lies differ from fantasy
or the magic in their world
that his flattening realism
will never dispel, the wonder

of dream. In a season of good cheer
a killer hurtles a truck
into a Berlin Christmas Markt,
Melbourne men plan murder

in the venerable name of God. Yet
in Gaoxiong's deeply Chinese streets
carols play, electric trees
twinkle: Christmas is spreading.

This Christmas, half a world
away from you, I will look up
and, cloudlessness or clouds,
will see the moon is there

and by some process I don't pretend
to understand, or will ever,
I feel, though too far off
you are yet almost beside me

and that corny, reflecting moon
will spread its determined light
on us both.

Reflection

When my partner, Annamaria Weldon, and I got together it was unexpected – we are both seniors and widowed – and I had already booked to travel to Gaoxiong in Taiwan for Christmas. My older son and his family, including my two young grandchildren, live there. Christmas isn't part of Taiwanese traditions but there are touches of it nowadays. I'm not a Christian but I've always liked the atmosphere that Christmas creates. I stayed alone in a room and met the family during the day. On Christmas Eve I listened to Dvorak's 'Song to the Moon' on YouTube; the lyrics are corny but in a song you can get away with that whereas in poetry you can't. So I tried to do so. The news events in the poem are actual news items from that time.

Dennis Haskell

Missing

Gail Hennessy

23rd April, 2020

on the way to pathology
an eeriness of absence
ghosts the suburbs

it's around 7am
early enough
for some traffic to be threading
the empty streets

there's plenty of parking and we stop
outside the centre where
the pavement's lined with closed
shop fronts some boarded up

the maw of the waiting room
yawns empty although
it is usually crowded
for these fasting tests

there's a bottle of sanitiser
on the counter and the receptionist
who's on her own checks the form

she ushers me to a chair in a small room
and straps a band tight around my arm
selects vials with caps of varied colours
I watch the needle ingest what seems
enough blood to leave me completely drained

though I know it's only a miniscule amount

she touches her name tag
inscribed with the name that links
her like an umbilical cord
to four generations of women

and tells me of her mother
in the nursing home nearby
who lights up when her new
great-granddaughter comes to visit

and I realise then how much I am
missing the kindness of strangers.

Reflection

I wrote this poem in mid-March 2021 almost a year to the day after we went into lockdown following the beginning of the pandemic.

I wanted to record something that came from that time when we were grieving for so much that was lost. My poem tells the story of the first time my husband and I went out after a month of Isolation. While it attempts to capture the eeriness of that time it more importantly tries to capture the important place ordinary day to day rituals play in our lives.

When I was growing up I was often embarrassed by my mother's propensity to talk to strangers. Although she was not an outgoing person my mother had a strong desire to belong and it is only now, as a senior person, do I recognise that trait in myself – the human need for connection.

The closing line of my poem echoes Blanche DuBois' words from Tennessee Williams' drama, *A Streetcar Named Desire*: 'I have always depended on the kindness of strangers'.

Gail Hennessy

Yunnan Golden Monkey Tea

Paul Hetherington

1.
Sulphur-crested cockatoos
shine like white dust
in the dark afternoon,
summer's muscularity
emboldened in their raucous bodies.
They plump feathers
against rain, breaking tips
from the ornamental pear,
while your intimate words
possess a quiet pungency—
as if we're pouring
Yunnan Golden Monkey tea
into glazed cups.

2.
Leaves that unfold and taper;
a colour like hair on a monkey's neck;
a malty smoothness; tannins that stretch
the length of the tongue.
You mix it with honey and a splash of milk
and it's a redolent puzzle—
how tea can suggest there's plentiful time
and a hand-picked place.

The cockatoos shriek at a storm
that moves in quickly from the west,
lifting from flexing branches
into a diving, skidding wind,
and canopies bustle—

like fingers on abacuses
counting down the placid days.

3.
The path's fractured sandstone
littered with the cockatoos' debris
might be a kind of cuneiform
writing the world's names—
as if grace were something
thrown on the ground
suddenly; or left in the air
as a screech's aftermath;
or etched in wranglings
and wearings of ancient stone;
or contained in first unfurling leaf
and gathered bud—
now curling in this proffered cup
like monkeys' paws.

Reflection

This is a contemporary reflection on the old idea that sharing tea
is a way of finding comfort or solace in the face of the world's
travails and uncertainties. I love Yunnan Golden Monkey Tea,
although I don't drink it very often—however, there are particular
moments when it seems to be called for. It is a drink I associate
with a certain attentiveness and quietude.

Paul Hetherington

Destinies

Daniel Ionita

You might remember that in the first of my destinies,
I was selling happiness to tourists,
like fairy floss at a crowded country fair
– they would open their mouths wide, take one bite,
and then throw it into the next rubbish bin.

Next,
I would transform,
suddenly and without apparent reason,
into a chubby Father Christmas
– always rushing around with a fed-up attitude –
to distribute toys Made in China
to all sorts of little twerps.
I pulled some horrid faces at them
when their parents were distracted elsewhere.
They would scream
that Father Christmas had scared them.
But the parents would soothe them,
explaining that, in fact…
Father Christmas does not exist!

At other times, I woke up
as a customs officer for thoughts and dreams,
charging duty
for all sorts of high-volume personal items –
from prayers to palaver, to pondering, to passion,
to purposes, promises, pleasure,
and everything else pertaining to human proclivities.
These were passing, planned or haphazardly,
through people's heads –

mine, yours, everybody's.
I stacked them in a folder
to be evaluated later,
at the Last Judgment.

In one of the more challenging of these destinies
I was waking up as a nocturnal clown,
with vast experience
into the amusement of your body.
Lately
I started introducing myself
as a professor of calligraphy,
in a sordid world where no one
uses pens anymore.
They were all laughing at me,
pounding on keyboards –
monotonous, abject, and deadly keyboards.

I now look at this ceiling … I am pricked with needles
like an inverted porcupine, a converted hedgehog.
Then I remembered you holding my hand on your last visit.
And I understood.
My destiny was not in playing Father Christmas,
nor being a customs officer, nor a professor of calligraphy.
These were just some things I did along the way.
My destiny lies in the sky above the ceiling.
Or maybe just in taking a nap in the afternoon.
Perhaps holding your hand one more time?
Most likely, it lies in all these things.

Reflection

The more time passes, the more I realise that my life is like a length of cloth, mostly woven from what seem to be mundane events – going to school, to work, educating children (mine and then others' – there was a misguided period when I thought I could achieve this...). In order of volume, for me, next in line are periods of suffering. I have not escaped them, though I tried to abscond by hopping from one country to another, from one end for the world to another – from my native (and at the time, totalitarian) Romania, to Austria, then to New Zealand, and now I'm calling Australia home. I found there is no escape. People much wiser than me understood this a lot earlier. Therefore, what I am trying now (and not always succeeding, though I do not give up!) is to engage with life as it is, embracing it with all it has to offer. Because I learned that almost entirely independent of my efforts, and often despite them – interwoven through all this boring or painful stuff – there are glimmer moments of grace, short bursts of eternity, glimpses of what we, lazily and almost off-handedly, call 'happiness'.

Daniel Ionita

Gloucester Tops Rain Forest

Linda Ireland

Here is a place that speaks in colours.
I hear its greens in shades that shake sounds
from soft shapes on quivering ferns
and licks of moss on the rain sheen
of fallen logs.

Doves, a flight in suddenness,
rise in a flush of grey feathers,
rattle and squeak,
feather-rabble monochrome.

Colour-sound even in silence,
even in heavy mush of brown leaf mulch
down where the silence is so moist
it is roll and lilt of muteness on the tongue.

The mist's breath is slow suck and puff
around pink lungs of fungi.
Everywhere asks in wet silence,
replies in dank stillness.

Beyond,
the nearest largest mountain,
a dark green stain,
strains for voice
amongst so much white whispering.

Muteness and lilt,
pitch of colours:
perfect.

Reflection

We all have a place that speaks to us on a very personal level, intimate, consoling. For me there is a special language in a rainforest. Here I retreat to unwind and read poetry, another 'place' which speaks to me. In this poem I have sought to mirror the sensual language of the rainforest in the richness of sounds and connotations which language offers in poetry. Words are but one form of language through which we interpret our world. Sometimes we see in words and hear in colours. Both the reading of poetry and being in the still sensuousness of a rainforest invite absorption and reflection. Poetry and rainforest share language, consolation, place.

Linda Ireland

Acorn

Ivy Ireland

Working this through, then,
in the freezer sits an oak seed.
Grant this disk of vital spark
true wintering, allow time
to do what time will:
take in a tiny death, magic it to
august life. Give it over to the quickening.
Pluck it out for planting in spring.
When the tree sprouts, this suspension,
this freezing over, this
nothing all the time empty
stillness –
what is nothing –
will have been one universal
instant, one essential
delay. Necessity. Nothing more.
Nothing less.
Don't smirk at this,
as though you do not need to be told.
As though that rule is now redundant,
as though your grief is more.
As though it were all so simple,
naming loss. Giving word to this
deep howl in the rotting moss forest.
As though it were human to
allow, after pause, life.
As though one could simply
mark the darks of solstice,
dutifully map the returning line of light
along the passage tomb floor, take

heed as ancestors all the while whisper,
'thus and so, thus and so,'
and navigate towards remedy.
As though you will ever
leave off your keening
for the sake of scientific fact.

Still. A life pod graces
the suburban kitchen freezer:
enforced cryonic suspension.
May cold hell hold enough deep magic
to fire the new shoot through.

Reflection

'Acorn' is a poem that isn't afraid to explore the deep darks in
order to arrive at a small kernel of hope. In writing this poem,
I was drawn to the central image of the small seed of the king
of trees, and the spark that arrives seemingly out of nowhere
to grant life to the seemingly inanimate. While the tone of
the poem might be at times dark, cold, or even abject, I sought
to capture the essence of renewal, the deep balm that might
arrive (again, seemingly out of nowhere) after periods of illness,
grief or loss. The sense of faith and resilience that can appear
in these trying times is almost paradoxical, ineffable, and yet it
is numinous.

Ivy Ireland

Touch

Andy Jackson

late winter, I can't work any longer
lie down beside you hollow on the long green
couch by the window

soon enough

they're back
settling on the rail of the deck
having figured by now we're no threat

two ravens

the black sheen of their feathers
absorbing all light, any myth
subtle clucks and murmurs between them

an eye on the blue
from where competition could swoop in

quietness and presence spill out
from their pure white eyes
across the trees, through the window

one bows her head, a gestured plea for touch

after a moment, he runs the point of his beak
in gentle, attentive circles across her scalp

                now there are no carrion
                no haunting caw

no omen of anything coming

only this bond
we sit within
afraid to move

how quickly tenderness can abandon us

Reflection

'Touch' was written during a period of fatigue and uncertainty. I'd found myself inside another wave of unresolved grief about being in my own body. It gets better over time, but it's cyclical, tumultuous. On top of that, we were in the wake of the 2019-20 Black Summer, in the middle of the Covid-19 hibernation. The ground under all our feet felt charred and unstable. What next? How to feel safe? How to belong?

Simply seeing one raven – a bird that we find hard to really see, because they're so common and erroneously associated with ill omen – give sensual, caring attention to another brought me back to earth, literally. These hard questions of suffering and community persist, but when we're open to tenderness, they soften a little.

Andy Jackson

Like a Butterfly

Judy Johnson

'Oh human race, born to fly upward,
wherefore at a little wind dost thou so fall' Dante

To be as a kite,
    some enabler
        of the air's imagination.

To know a loss of meaning
as the lifting off
    of a heaviness

we have carried all the way
    from the catacomb of the womb.

To forget it was determined
    we would become
        a spined and serious book

instead of two
    identical fly leaves
        opening and closing
            on a delicate hinge.

To disregard the gravitas that anchors
        the language of spirit
            to the page of bone.

To push upwards on the screeking panes
        of wordless fears that multiply in our heads.

To let the breeze
of the closest thing we need to paradise
enter, mute but for its fragrant sighs

Reflection

An antidote to what ails us has always been to lose ourselves in
the natural world. We have much to learn from other creatures
who live in the moment unaware that death is looming. But-
terflies have very short lives, but every minute is heightened,
expansive and full of purpose with no fear to taint the experi-
ence of being utterly present.

Judy Johnson

Our mother/our father

Sue Joseph

Our mother's place
in that space
at the centre of our family home
is no longer hers;

her heart
(our burning sun)
at the heart of our family.

She is gone.

But in her leaving a
renewal/repair/rebirth.
(ancient mythic magic).
Rediscovery;
unthinkable, really.

Unimaginable.

For over there, our father:
holding her hand every day,
witnessing this demise;
this disintegration;
guiding her;
feeding her;
seeing her.
Deep caring.

Returning home,
enfolded by her vacated

space/her place;
her scent;
her absent presence.

Our father endures a slow,
throbbing ache;
psychic violence
crafting/grasping
life from fragments of hers;
from the fracturing existence of a wife;
of a life
(more than six decades).

We realise:
his burning tenderness;
his despair;
his scorching anger;
his sorrow
pervading that place/
her space;

and then this,
a fresh dynamic:
deep conversations;
time spent with him,
and only him;
daily chats,
in her space/in her place;
kindnesses offered
and accepted.
Laughter.
His stories,
untold,
quietly, surprisingly,
remembered and recounted.

Tears; many tears
(too many tears).

Gentleness shifts seeming censorious silences;
Phoenixlike affinities/
harmonies arise from
her fiery,
ashy
wreckage.

Sustaining,
now she is gone from
this place/
her space.

Holding up/
upholding him in his grief
(and us).

Endowing.

This,
her binding bequest.

Reflection

The loss of our mother in 2019 through Alzheimer's disease was devastating, as were the years leading to her death. Our father always said he would never have her in a nursing home, but this decision was taken out of his hands for 16 months before she passed.

Every day, he visited and sat by her side, mostly silent, holding her hand.

I have written three grieving artefacts regarding our mother's death. Two essays and a poem: 'Disappearing: Abyssal lines of ageing, a personal eco-story', (*Axon: Creative Explorations*, 2019); 'Suspension' (*Antipodes, 2018);* and 'Alcoves' (*On First Looking*, 2018).

I always thought I was done, until receiving this invitation. This poem is inspired by the conclusion of the 2019 essay. It was a fraught experience, writing that essay, appropriating Robert Nixon's theory of Slow Violence (2013) as analogy for the demise of elders suffering Alzheimer's. It is an angry essay, and I felt the conclusion seemed too neat; too hopeful; too trite. But I left it there because it intuitively wrote itself, and is true: in the loss of our mother, we re-discovered our father.

And it was an epiphany.

And now it is a poem.

Thank you.

Sue Joseph

thoughts post-diluvian

Kit Kelen

in the after fall
breeze brushed to drip

how bright the green
leafs up to blue

and all forever's with
just as long as it lasts

as if the kiss
still on the lip

all glory
pent up, much to say

light for a revelation –
everyone shining inside with it

listen for a next come-down
smell the ants come out

and so the dark is seen aside
the forest in the song

you couldn't paint a world this way
but this is the one to save

Reflection

It's been wet. Wet's better than the fires. Or it's easy to say from the side of a hill. The fires felt as if one were being caught up with. The floods are more like the world keeping arm's length away. I feel that *the daily kit* has been turning into a weather report lately. But there's much philosophy in the weather. And poetry and politics. Weather and shelter and what have we done? We live in an Age of Weather now, though perhaps it's yet to be declared. The time for politeness about the weather has passed. We need to own it – joys, griefs, all. To take action. We need to report the weather inside as well. One of poetry's great duties is witness. So we witness the where and when we live. And how we happen to be here. What we can and won't forgive. We need to rouse hearts to this cause – to trip up greed, to love life, love this planet. To witness the weather we're under. Guess how to get over. How to be part of the bettering.

Kit Kelen
iii.21

The Spaghetti Maker

Jean Kent

In her hands, this stilled
sunlit wave. We place our order for pizza and slightly
turning see her ...

Spaghetti streams from the machine
and she holds it like hair, wheat-blonde, wet-combed,
long lazy strands

from the scalp of a child
or someone ill.

Soon we will walk talcum-shadowed
under melaleucas flaking their filo bark.
On a bitumen hill,

snow gulls with red-hot beaks
will melt, watching our fingers fill

with teased gold cheese, warm dough
and a predatory perfume of prawns ...

We will join a glitter of lunchtime pausers,
parked like an audience at a broad daylight drive-in —

all feeding on the sight of sea

blissed blue-green-turquoise — an ocean opening itself
industriously smashing its sparkle
then calming back

into something huge and whole again.

But first: we pause with pasta. Here, under a stucco sky,
Chianti bottles are basketed in dust —
but in the woman's hands, sun-on-water sets.

Like a swooping bird her scissors slowly

snip the loopy light. She scoops it all towards her, then
settles its swirling life like a boneless wing
on a bench to dry …

Outside in the sun the day is proving,
rising sweetly ordinary

as she begins again   again
to embrace whatever the still

steel offers —

to comb out to air this gold,
to coax it into her arms and to fill
our watching with these drooping, resting waves

until
she has comforted as much as she can hold.

Reflection

'The Spaghetti Maker' began as a bonus that came with a take-away pizza. Just inside the door of Don Beppino's Restaurant, a woman was slowly making spaghetti, while we waited for the pizza to cook. She sat there in a space of such silent calm, I felt as I had stumbled into a Vermeer painting. A very ordinary day in Newcastle suddenly became charmed, graced with unexpected beauty and hope. As I was writing the poem, I tried to give the lines the same lilting and falling rhythms that made the woman's simple work so calming to watch. The poem's ending took me by surprise! But the whole experience was a gift of comfort. I hope that my poem is, too.

Jean Kent

A Personal History of Joy

Andy Kissane

'*… and once more saw the stars.*'
—*Dante Alighieri*

It hangs for a moment before your face—
a dandelion puff, a sheaf of smoke, wonder
before its vanishing, your exhaled breath hovering
above floodlit shadows, the lapping oval
which in winter, after heavy rain, resembles
the viscous crema on top of an espresso,
its aroma lifting, bitterness lingering on your tongue,
the caffeine hit like the exhilarating shock of an idea
that comes to you anywhere, at any time—
while digging in the vegetable patch, say,
feeling for the familiar globular solidity of a potato—
Otway Reds, glorious Dutch Creams, the pink blotches
of a King Edward that you've renamed 'Goughs',
after Edward Gough Whitlam who believed in free
university education and the cultivation of all people,
no matter how much of a spud they appeared to be.

I love how we live in sensual, sensing bodies,
how when I spy the pied cormorant lurking
on the mangrove flat, then hear the flapping of wings
and look back to see that the bird has gone, I still
have a nanosecond of its presence in my head,
along with all kinds of ephemera: how as a teenager
I would dress up in my mother's stockings
because they were as close as I could get
to the scent of a woman; how diving under waves
I hear the endless rhapsody of the sea; how
walking in an angophora forest I can believe that trees

pass on their wisdom in ways we are just beginning
to understand. Recently, while roasting chicken thighs
with Jerusalem artichokes and banana shallots,
I discovered the miracle of the marinade—drowning
the pieces in a baste of olive oil, tarragon, thyme,
crushed pink peppercorns and saffron threads,
then tossing everything together until my hands
were stained yellow, the bowl a fragrant, rustic promise.

I suspect that the unmarinated life is not worth
living, that the neural pathways need to be lit
by all kinds of sources—the glow of a desk lamp
illuminating an open book, the sudden flashing
of fireflies intent on attracting a mate, the vivid streamers
of a city street captured by time-lapse photography.
In *River*, the grieving detective is visited by manifests
who talk of the lives they once shared,
just as I glimpse my father sitting on the verandah
sipping a beer, or raising the lid of the barbecue
as the swirling smoke weaves around his outstretched arm.
If you are lucky there's a twist in the tale and everything
coheres, is graced with a meaning that never seemed
possible, so when you're swung in the tackle
and thrown face-down into the mud, you lift
your head in time to see the ball spinning end over end
right over the man dressed in a white butcher's coat,
and even though thirty-five years have passed,
you can still remember how he glances in your direction
and greets your clumsy snap with a two-thumbed salute,
a perfect accompaniment to the endorphin light that swamps
your mind as you rise again into the shining world.

Reflection

For a while now, I have been experimenting with poems that start somewhere and end—well, I never really know where they will end exactly, and that for me is the joy of writing them. Poetry has the capacity to celebrate joy and happiness in a way that fiction rarely does. Perhaps this is because the best poetry sings, but it is also because happiness in a novel tends to be boring. So fiction is often concerned with loss, misery and despair. Even the ultimate example of a happy character, Levin, from Tolstoy's *Anna Karenina* spends much of the novel desperately searching for the elusive meaning of his life.

Reading this poem a few years after I wrote it, I now see that it is also about the life of the mind, how a mind can go anywhere, from the republican renaming of a potato, to the flight of a waterbird, and onto the memory of my father standing over a barbeque. It begins with an exhaled visible breath on a winter's evening and ends with an invisible held-breath as the football sails over the goal umpire's head. As a history of joy, it is imperfect, it leaves so much out, but I hope it might lead you to reflect on the power of your own mind and the joy in your life.

Andy Kissane

Breath

Shari Kocher

As when walking yesterday's
catastrophic dawn, the surf
a cauldron turned wild and brown,
two pelicans rowed the air like floating
parentheses and swept with purpose
the high, sweet, cold-fronted wind.
I want nothing less than to be
blessed by poems such as these
that breathe with the soul's hands
and feet. As when I lay my hands
on a woman's back and she lets
out a breath like a dreaming forest
and I feel the sky step
toward her as she lets, without labour,
her breath back in. As when her
trapezius flutters like a manta ray
coming to stillness in the dozing depths,
and I feel the breath she lets roll through her,
the full winged scapular
softenings that open her rhomboids
like flowers. As when the deer
decides it is safe to step
into her very own
moonfresh meadow
through the velvet, permissible dark,
there on the underbreath I follow
without sight, by touch alone, the deep
heart's mysterious rose, the rare
treasures it lifts from the very back
of the heart that hardly gets touched,

or not enough, oh, there, at last, at long
last, the deer remembers
how to drink the tenderest dew
in that moonwashed and radiant field.

Reflection

This poem arrived on the wind with a pair of pelicans who flew
in so close over my head one early morning beach walk that I
felt a rush of what seemed like their united, rhythmic breathing
upon me. It was a significant morning, and I was grateful for
their company, gliding back and forth, for the whole length of
an intentional *what-shall-I-do?* beach-walk, from Bar Beach to
Little Redhead Point in Newcastle, during the first week of the
catastrophic bush fires of 2019–2020. These fires were causing
so much air pollution that matters of breath and easy breathing
were literal and pressing concerns for me at the time, though
I had been tracking both the literal and metaphoric power of
breath in my remedial massage practice for some time. In a
wordless way, this poem arrived as a gift. I did not shy away
from its lyricism, nor its saturation in the implicit testing of
the many ways that beauty heals. There is a tenderness in this
poem that defies the critical faculties I also bring to bear in both
my remedial and poetic practices, yet in this poem, and in the
face of climate catastrophe, something in me gave way. Paying
witness to vulnerability, as much as to the wordless rush of spirit
those two pelicans gifted me that day, I dedicate this poem to all
that the life-affirming act of breathing allows.

Shari Kocher

A Peaceful Room

Richard Lander

The painting by an ancestor past
Myrtleford eucalypts and a cool mountain stream
Seen through English eyes, not quite real

The gentle tick-tock of a gingerbread clock
Sits on a bookcase of wind-thrown kauri
Counting down the seconds of a happy life
Kauri as smooth as oil and almost as old

Ornaments abound in this peaceful room
Elegant flamenco dancer in blue, bell-bottomed dress
Arms outstretched as graceful as an eagle in flight

Crystal decanters hold whisky in their poisonous embrace
Large bowls rest easily on Italian coffee table
Exhibiting the potter's art, thrown with the same love
With which this peaceful room was created

Ancient etchings of a man in vest coat and tie
A mouse scurrying over learned books
Others of valley tracks and mountain trees

A native coolamon artfully patterned with poker work
Lies beside carved boab seed with images of kangaroo,
Emu, snakes and warriors
Amijangal pyrography at its very best

Aboriginal paintings on two walls
One a dreamtime image in the reds, yellows and greys
Of ancient Northern Territory coastal land

Gaunt black and white mimi figures carrying dilly-bags
Filled with octopus, barramundi and shellfish
Each spiked with thin tecoma vine spears
To feed their hungry tribe

Lamps throw a soft glow on special treasures
Grandfather's antique lawyer bookcase
Chicago-made from golden American oak

Family keepsakes make this a special room
A room for reflection and contemplation
A room for reading, understanding and quiet talk
A peaceful room

Reflection

My home, like most people's homes, is my castle. Although I
spend many hours behind my desk each day, either writing or
researching, or simply paying bills, when I really want to switch
off and to relax, the room I withdraw to is our lounge room.
Lyndall, my wonderful wife of more than 50 years, has made
this a delightfully peaceful room, soft to the eye, and easy on the
mind – a place to be completely comfortable, to totally unwind
and to reflect, to enjoy some of our collected memories and to
come away fully refreshed.

Richard Lander

Jack

Martin Langford

i.m. John 'Jack' Adams 1905-1988

He would dress in the darkness,
and make his way down
through the echoes and gleams of the Yard:
climb into floorlessness –
crouch there, aloft and adrift,
while he soldered ships' brains.

Those were the days of class warfare –
of Dads who would not put
one ha'penny down
lest their sons became better than they.

Nothing for tutoring:
You didn't tell me he charged!

Nor for his music:
his Communist father would keep
the piano Jack bought – and that only he played.

So he took on more pupils
while plaster Olympians
frowned at the earnest, wrong man.

And he kept up his speed –
while the metronome laughed.

And he wore gloves at work
so his eloquent fingers
would not be ashamed in clean rooms.

But then war, with its moraines for choices.

And the years, after that, of hard peace.

So he never became a conductor.

How could a dockyardie
ever become a conductor?

All he could do
was to make what he could of it:
leaven – with working-class zen –
his difficult journey to dance-steps –
a progress for grief and good cheer –
like Beethoven's brave allegretto.

Reflection

Jack Adams was my grandfather. He was an electrician's assistant in the Plymouth (UK) dockyards, before the war. Somehow, as a boy, he developed a passion for music. He was never going to be able to give this the focus it needed, however, and after many setbacks (his father insisting on keeping his piano, the depression, the war) he had to come to terms with the fact that he would never realise his ambitions. What has stayed with me, lifelong, is the dignity and strength with which he accepted this.

When I searched for an image which might capture his note of acceptance and good cheer, I thought of the allegretto of the Beethoven Seventh. I have always found the tone of this movement ambiguous: sometimes it seems filled with grief; at other times, it has an irrepressible forward momentum. It is the same ambiguity I sensed in my grandfather: he quietly carried the weight of a great disappointment, but he never allowed that to interfere with his capacity to enjoy life, or to carry himself in an upbeat and even-tempered manner.

I selected this poem because I think many people dealing with illness find themselves in a similar place – and often deal with it in a similarly courageous fashion: they may privately be confronting great difficulties, yet they often insist on maintaining a steady and even cheerful manner. There is strength and acceptance in this, and also, I think, an element of gift for the people around them.

Martin Langford

The Homecoming

Andrew Lansdown

1
Restraint

As the car pulls up
the pup goes prancing to the door
to greet my grandkids.
Though I stay put, I too feel like
yapping and rolling on the floor.

2
Anticipation

I hear the dog greet
my grandchildren in the drive.
Shortly, they'll enter
my study with jostle and shove
and paw at me for scraps of love.

Reflection

Two things came together to move me to write 'The Homecoming'.
First, my wife, Susan, and I were looking after our grandchildren
in their own home while their parents were overseas. Second, a
close friend, Hal Colebatch, died and his widow, Alexandra, asked
me to conduct his funeral service and to deliver the eulogy. While
working on the eulogy one afternoon, I heard the children's dog go
berserk with excitement as Susan drove into the carport, bringing
the children home from school. And, like the dog, I felt a flood of
anticipation and happiness, emotions so at odds with the ones I had
just been experiencing. I immediately felt an urge to try to capture
some sense of this joy, this gladness, in poetry. So I began work
on several short poems—poems modelled on the ancient Japanese
poetic form known as the tanka (or waka), which consists of 31
syllables arranged in five lines of 5, 7, 5, 7, 7 syllables respectively.
Over the next few days, I wrote half-a-dozen tanka, and finally
settled on the two that now sit together to comprise the poem, 'The
Homecoming'.

Andrew Lansdown

Uncut pages

Penelope Layland

Salvaged from his relic things,
I iron my father's handkerchiefs.

I iron them as my mother did:
squared flat in two balletic sweeps
then folded—swept—folded—swept—

a closing out of the just-lived week,
a making, from its small remains,
provisions for the next.

Gulp of steam, hot cotton swoon,
a rhythmic rock on naked heels,
a pleasure in precision.

Stacked and cooling in my drawers,
the best, least-frayed, are kept for worst—
the days when it is dark by noon.

The rest, for fleeter days like this,
small books with uncut pages where
all my thanks is written.

Reflection

I love my collection of threadbare men's cloth handkerchiefs. They once belonged to my father, and they remind me not only of him, but of the importance of small, unflashy things, of the calm pleasure that can be taken in routine tasks, and of thankfulness, even if it is unwritten.

Penelope Layland

elegy for a type of youth

Lynette Lounsbury

here is the old young heart
here is the wild antique
this is where the cup was full
and words were the bright lips
of a gibbous moon
here were the parched vessels
of a thirsty soul
the raised hand of a face
yet to see death,
the brave feet of a voice
yet to whisper discontent
to a dwindling wind.
hope without stillness,
mirth without wisdom,
candour without compassion,
tentative truths on a tentative tongue

flinging smiles at dangerous strangers
walking alone through the dark

farewell the old young heart

Reflection

'Elegy for a type of youth' is my farewell to one of my selves, to one version of my young heart. It is a remembrance for a time of unknowing optimism and questioning, but also of a time of fear and cautious self-assertion. It is an acknowledgement that our former selves were beautiful in their fresh ignorance and that we can say goodbye to them with affection rather than grief.

Lynette Lounsbury

Autumn

Win Luben

Thick, green moss paving the sloping ground
Red, black and white koi in a pool
Granite rocks sparkling in the sunlight
Red maple leaves falling softly down
The red tide flowing slowly down the slope

Please do not hurry, please do not hurry.

Reflection

My father loved learning languages and worked on ships which enabled him to travel the globe. I inherited his love of languages and other cultures. I wrote this poem in the *New Leaves* writing group led by Judith Beveridge and Carolyn Rickett as I wanted to share my experience of travelling to Japan. I hope this poem is an invitation to live more mindfully in the present and to appreciate the richness of simplicity.

Win Luben

Balcony

Greg McLaren

I was standing on the hotel balcony,
wrapped in and warped by the fat tropical air
falling through quickening dusk and

the ocean – azure, opaline daylight –
edging its way across the pale thin strand
that must once have been a beach.

The salty heat. The pressing on my chest.
My slick skin, the pattering pulse just inside
that film. The palms along the esplanade nod a little,

almost swaying, woozy kids.
Seabirds out of sight creak and sigh, crark
and snip. Little prints, I suppose, that the tide

covers up, where its broad flail reaches.
Condensation on the glass door from the aircon,
tarnished chrome on the outdoor

furnishings. Flaps and strips from the awning
flicker, sharp tongues hissing, snap at the wind.
The sound of cars up and down the strand

under all this, the tracery of headlights now as dark
really starts to slip onto itself. Voices, some
a little urgent, a question, going on the tone.

The smoke's from rainforest inland, burning
at last, after long memory's eternal wet.
A shiver, of a sudden, from whatever bug

is seesawing through me.
You're stirring, a bit, in the bed,
the thermostat working hard to prevail,

the whole slant stumble and trip on the spiral stair,
the giddy glance down the mine shaft,
the tip of a small stone into the long well.

Reflection

'Balcony' isn't exactly the most comforting or consoling of
poems. Its roots, I suppose are in part what seems a current
occupation with the effects of climate change, already visible
but projected into an imagined near future, and an engagement
with Chaise Twichell's great poem 'The Whirlpools', from her
book *The Ghost of Eden*, which revolves around not dissimilar
concerns. The world known by the speaker is toppling, coming
apart—the sea is rising, the land is burning, they're sick and
the air con is on the blink. If anything, this poem is offered out
of empathy, out of shared(ish) experience, which might be the
only relative comfort to be had, given what's clearly unfolding.

Greg McLaren

frost at morning

Chris Mansell

it is a clear cold morning
and this day you know
your dreams have been fulfilled
you sit in a blue carpeted room
in the sun reading
the old Chinese poets
with a tea at your side
such delicate amnesia
and all the world
has converged
for your ravishment

yesterday you
delighted in praise
not of your own
book but of one
you love
– though you've never met –
her translucent lines
poems as bright
and pearly as frost

and in this dream
today this truth
you work you own
modest icicles
the radio mumbling
in the background
the sun on your feet
you are ill broke widowed

disenfranchised but
in love

these words your
dancing paramours
your ice clear pleasures
the particles of snow you
hold in your mouth

Reflection

This is a love poem really – to the day, sunlight, poetry, love itself, the sheer pleasure of small things. It was a freezing day and I'm sitting in the only warm spot in the house (on the floor) reading and thinking about the favourite poets, new and ancient, who have gifted their poems to us. Of course, 'Frost at Morning' speaks to Coleridge's 'Frost at Midnight'. Coleridge speaks of his little baby. He imagines the child wandering 'like a breeze/by lakes and sandy shores... [where] thou shalt see and hear/the lovely shapes and sounds intelligible/of that eternal language'. What a gift! Breathing in life. 'Frost at Morning' is at the other end of life, where I feel that I have been blessed, despite every obstacle (and there were quite a few!) I had that lovely thing that Coleridge wished for his baby: to breathe in the world, to delight in the languages of nature and of people; to experience the amazement of being alive. Those icicles at the end of the poem are brief but exquisite. Small things, it turns out, are not small things.

Chris Mansell

The Unseen River

Lizz Murphy

Bandannas swirl saffron on lotus white necks

A small girl wears soft floral cotton
is a tender garden
is her own hunkering island
Coiling waves separate her features

Her father at the top of the alley sits against
a gull-grey wall legs rippling forward ankles crossed
like the meeting tides A white spread cloth is a chant
marigolds yellow and tangerine its garlands

Intense eyes elaborate eyes gold red green kohl-lined

Everyone preparing for Devi Saraswati
Shrines emerging turquoise on street stalls
footpaths and kerbs Incense berries flowers
pressed on the palimpsest of the festive city

Shrines like theatrettes Life-size goddesses
bone-beautiful faces under fabric canopies caressed
into sunrays illuminated in major streets and lanes
tributaries that might suddenly change course

The goddess transported by the dozen is placed
regally along both sides of an open truck
Flamboyant workers off to fragrant fields She cuts
a blaze through traffic sings my breath in her wake

Sculpted hands and wrists slender as swan heads

The girl's father grower of the mango moon
and mandarin sun festoons adorning the shrines
calls to his daughter giddy with her making
Riverruns in her head currents playing her fingers

She transforms a broken shoebox with tape and scraps
builds herself a school its bell her bronze nightingale
Dedicated afternoon mothers Vendors with lime
lemon fairy floss in plastic squares along amber canes

She builds her own city store to sell sarees
of shimmering riverwater eddies of colour
nets of glistening fish Earth spice monsoon
Riverstones glinting like rings in a silty display

She builds a ferry to travel her unseen Ganga Ma
take her dolphin-dream dip grow her dorsal fin
swash her flukes in a salvation shandy of life unlife
riverbanks braised in worship and woodsmoke

Reflection

'The Unseen River' was written after the first of two swift visits to Calcutta, on poetry tours coinciding with the Calcutta Book Fair, where 2.5 million people willingly queue to buy books and meet authors.

I chose this poem as it is dense with colour and activity and reflects the joy of the celebration of Devi Saraswati, goddess of learning, arts and music. It was such a gift to be there during that festive time.

Of course, Calcutta was also challenging. From the landing of the guest house it sounded overwhelmingly chaotic and standing on the kerb outside it looked it. You soon learn though, that there is some system to it all. People notice when others want to 'push on' and make way; taxies fold their mirrors in and skim past each other with skill; locals halt streams of traffic to cross the road … and generously usher others along with them.

There are by far, more confronting things than traffic and crowds, but that's for another time. Instead here is the moment I cherish the most – on this busy, broken pavement, a small girl imagining and making to her heart's content.

Lizz Murphy

Letter to a Dead Parent

David Musgrave

Whenever I look at your grandson,
I see dad's face, but you're the one
or several parts of one, who animates his rage
and cheek, just as how the other day
at two-and-a-quarter, he put a soccer ball
into a bucket and called it 'ice cream', licking it.
It's as if you're still alive, but blind to survival,
counting 'one, two, five, eighteen, twenty four'
with the precision of a train timetable,
opened at random. How you would have loved
to see him, even in your last unravelling,
the way he pushes away my hand
if I try to turn the page too soon, or how
he will stare blankly ahead, deaf to anything
I say before slyly looking sideways at me,
then laughing. This week I've drawn
fifty seven big fish and three hundred
and forty two little fish and thirty eight
spouting whales. It's hard to believe
that part of me could go on being, let alone
this tenacious chain that links to you, here,
where a breeze bends the corridor
around its cold and touches your hair.
A lot has happened since you've gone:
this pandemic; it's strange how there
are no individuals, just a society where
you can hide but can't run.
Your grandson brings me a horse's head
in the palm of his hand, separated from its body
by an accident, and overcome by penitence,

says 'sorry daddy' over and over, lying face down
on the ground. I didn't teach him this,
so where did he learn it? I'm sorry that you never got to see
his frown, breathing over a shark or Boss Boonga
in the Big House at the end of the road.
But when he points at agave plants
along the side path, tells me 'dinosaur'
I dine on sores, or dining saws remind me
of the older truths, the hardening of bone
or its mirror, sagging skin, a voice that's broken
into words, or words flowering into the wave
of a hand, 'goodbye outside, goodbye diningsaur'.

Reflection

This poem was written in response to a few things, some obvious, some not so. In 2019 I was invited to be part of *Notes from a Biscuit Tin*, which was a year-long project to commemorate and celebrate the philosophical and poetic vision of Mary Midgley on the centenary year of her birth. Midgley was a significant moral philosopher, influenced by Wittgenstein, who compared philosophy to plumbing — an image playfully conjured to tease those who would rather picture themselves as purveyors of luxury goods than tradesmen. In the *Notes from a Biscuit Tin* project, poets were asked to pair with philosophers and discuss a theme that related to an aspect of Midgley's work, and the poet was asked to contribute a poem which would later be lodged in the Durham University archives.

I was paired with David Macarthur and we responded to 'scientism', which is that cultural attitude which assumes that scientific knowledge and techniques should form the basis of most areas of knowledge, and which was critiqued in Midgley's book *Science and Poetry*. Midgely was critical of the atomistic myth, the notion that human 'sciences' could have their knowledge systems reduced to fundamental, invariant units, and also Margaret Thatcher's statement that there is no such thing as society, just individual men and women, and their families.

In the context of the COVID-19 pandemic, this atomistic notion of individualism seemed quaint, if not dangerous. While it was not the spark for this poem, it seemed a natural fit for the sense of sadness that accompanied the birth of my son when his grandparents, who would dearly have loved to see him, were no longer around. In this way, the sense of continuity and connection which the poem evinces acts as a counterweight to the myth of individualism and its atomistic roots, even in the face of personal loss and broader devastation.

David Musgrave

Zachary and the Angel

Jan Owen

When Zachary came to stay and
smashed the terracotta angel on a stone and
ran and hid, being only three,
my grandmother opened her eyes again
and smiled and drew me back through years of sun
as though to brush my hair, outside on the lawn.
Zachary pressed, breath held, against a wall,
his *What if?* gone to bits –
hands and wings strewn under the birdbath
cupped to heaven were evidence and warning
'So' would soon descend.

My grandmother set the hairbrush on the grass,
Don't get in such a tizz!
patiently teasing out a knot
as my heart went yes no yes
(I'd broken a second-best plate)
in time with small wild Zachary poised for flight,
his face like sunlight blotted out.
Off you go and play, drawing my blonde hairs
out of the brush, *I'll fix that blessed plate.*
Least said, soonest mended.

When Zachary fell asleep
I mixed the Araldite claggy
and eased the first wing back,
a swimming together, a tiny abrasion
then instant rapport, the intimate pleasure
of matchmaking an almost perfect fit,
or patching a quarrel up, head, hand and heart.

The cracks shone pinkly as proud flesh.

And the darker path of repair that
zigzagged over the willow-pattern bridge
would be the very strongest part
my grandmother said with a serious nod.
Next day, Zachary's wide-eyed start –
the cherub, miraculously intact,
perched back on the rim of the bowl.

He watched and watched the juggle of wrens
turn water to light.

Reflection

I think we owe a great deal to the example of grandparents. Besides the family rituals, it's often little details or everyday incidents in our grandparents' home that wait deep down in memory to unexpectedly surface. In my case, something broken, something mended, evoked a sense of my grandmother's presence, her dry humour and kindness, and her patience in managing my impulsiveness as a child. She understood curiosity and haste can leave some damage in its wake: a crybaby doll dismembered to find the voice box, a dropped willow pattern plate. So when my own grandchild Zachary tested his strength against a small terracotta angel I reacted as she would have. I was amused at the parallels, and in writing the poem I decided to include a flashback to childhood, drawing on a particular memory of Nanna – after all we had the same name now! It was the oddest pleasure to make a little word link between my grandmother and a great great grandson she never knew. I hope that you, dear reader, will smile as you read this, maybe thinking of your own grandparents or grandchildren, or both, and that you will be reminded of the ongoing bond between generations.

Jan Owen

Fishing with Seamus

Moya Pacey

(i.m. Charlie Brady 1918–1991)

Lured by the pull of your voice,
you hook me to the weight
of my father, born in that town
in the gabled house that stood
by the bridge, that arched
the clear waters of his boyhood.
The Moyola river, where he stepped
stones laid for an easy crossing,
or stood on the muddy bank
to flick a line and reel
in a fat, brown trout.
Seamus, you shoal words my way,
like the steady flow of mackerel
running with the tide. I feel,
the tug of the silver harvest,
'catch *my* heart off guard,
                    and blow it open.'

Note
'catch the heart off guard, and blow it open.' *Postscript,* Seamus Heaney

Reflection

Poetry is a mysterious art and I can't say why I wrote this poem except that I love Seamus Heaney's poetry and my father ebbs and flows in my memory.

My father was born in Castledawson, Northern Ireland, and lived there until his mother died when he was eight years old. His life changed utterly then.

Heraclitus said 'You cannot step into the same river twice.' Life, like the flow of a river, is constantly changing. But a poet can stay the flow of time. I can gift my father a return to the place where he was happiest. To a day spent fishing. A day when his mother is at home in the gabled house waiting for him. He will return with a gift for her. A fat brown trout.

Seamus Heaney has given me much consolation and solace in his poetry and, by coincidence, he grew up in Bellaghy on the other side of the Moyola River from Castledawson. Many of his poems use the imagery of water. In this poem, I acknowledge him and his poetry by using the epiphanic line from his poem 'Postscript' as the final line in my poem.

Moya Pacey

Coloratura

Geoff Page

Who says dogs don't speak Italian?
Research informs me that there are no

roles for dogs in opera
although today a fine soprano

from the front seat of my car
displayed a lengthy eloquence

of seven canine octaves which
encompassed her profound offence

at being left while I take coffee
in a swank espresso bar

blithely chatting with my friends
while she sings solo in the car.

Beyond the range of human hearing
at pitches only angels reach

(in tempi marked *adagio)*
when they're lilting each to each

with heavenly embellishments
unheard on earth outside Milano

she plied me with her wild dynamics,
fortissimo to coy *piano.*

Admittedly, her accent was
a tad Jack Russell here and there

but certainly she sang Italian,
creating levels of despair

that gradually grew more convincing,
right down to a final tremor.

Content among the legs of chairs,
she offers comments on the *crema*.

Reflection

'Coloratura' is about a friend's Jack Russell, Chilli, with whom my partner, Gwen, and I go walking early most mornings. On one occasion she was left with us for the weekend while her owners were out of town. We planned a coffee with other friends after our Saturday walk but Chilli set up such an eloquent ruckus that we decided to take her along in person and sit at an outside table. I hadn't known dogs could be so expressive.

Geoff Page

Molonglo Water (Jerrabomberra Wetlands)

Anita Patel

It's not the ocean that holds my heart
though I have walked at its unending edge ...
It's not the clamour of waterfalls—that muscular
tumble of cascading white though I have
bathed in pools of emerald light ...

It's simply ... a glimpse of reed and ripple—
shadow mottled glimmer beneath a Canberra sky—
colour of earth and leaf water—filled with frog song
and webbed feet—swoop of beak and wing water
spilling into billabong, swamp and creek—
been there forever water— stories to tell water—
Molonglo water ... washing
        every corner of my dusty heart ...

Reflection

This is poem of gratitude for the Jerrabomberra Wetlands where I walked, every day, during the months of lockdown in 2020. At a time when the world as we knew it changed drastically, life in the wetlands went on as usual. I watched birds and insects go about their daily business; I listened to grass rustle and frogs in reeds; I noticed lichen on seedpods and the scent of damp earth. All around me was the shimmer and sound of water (from the Molonglo River) in swamps, creeks, streams and billabongs.

The unchanging natural rhythms of this serene landscape offered real solace during those uncertain and stressful early months of the pandemic. I couldn't travel to exotic locations, eat at restaurants or see family and friends – but I could visit this tranquil refuge (so close to home) and splash my heart with Molonglo water.

Anita Patel

The Travel of Air

Phyllis Perlstone

It's a wet road
I can hear the rush
on black

on water splashing
on tyres running –
working at night

in the glamour
of car-lights
slowing brightly across the window –

no stars   I would inhale stars
their air   the space
they arc over us   their unreachable brightness

though I know
there's no air
no breath there –

a longer wheel of a car
passes through   goes softly
touching the rain

a faster car throwing the splashes
off
deserts the street

this morning
the traffic of rain has gone
into sun

the difference
as if I had space –
the distance has sounds   even

in the clear travel of air
in a small walk
the rush is my breath in the trees that I pass

Reflection

I wrote the 'The Travel of Air' as a sort of antidote to living in the
city (Sydney) on a rainy night – a bit hemmed in by city lights
and all that's artificial about the confinement that keeps our senses
quiet. I thought of being in the out-of-doors on a clear night away
where no electric lights doused the high beauty of the stars. Then
next, thinking of all the sounds I recognised outside the room and
its window I was sitting near, I was able to get some sense of life
beside my own – even if it was only cars in the rain.

The next morning of course was sunny, and everything I felt
was freer and I was more alive hearing my own breath as I walked
unconfined and untrammelled by thoughts – even of unreachable
illusions of brightness.

I chose this poem that it might arouse delight for the senses in
others confined for different reasons. In ill-health or immobility,
the reader might think of how it would be for them to get up on a
sunny day – even if it was winter – to be able to hear the sound of
their own breath as they went out among trees they passed.

Phyllis Perlstone

One for sorrow

Felicity Plunkett

Beside
me, the lone tern's composure shows
a foam-legged way forward. The sea draws
back its jostle and rush. Long
division —

space
between past and next. Each step
flossed and washed, I pace myself to walk
with you, fold my hunger small. I'm beyond
retreating —

beneath
the thought. Double-summering, the Arctic
tern crests long days' light, more
than we imagine in these dim hours,
yours —

alone
though I post pockets of song, packets
of tea, letters of hope: migratory,
achy, pecked at by our uncertain
tern.

Brace
myself. Stay, stacking words in the wrong
order — scale of lost notes, low
key — trying all the locks, love's
furious

                tenacity —
like the sea's one yacht — a dot. You're on its storm
-sloshed deck. Can't stand alone, so have to
crawl, clamber each waveturn's
jolt —

                upright
shore-staggering through sea's hustle
and shush. Disturbance swells and breaks
all night, its lullaby the hand
still —

                there
beside our cribbed and swaddled selves,
humming *Still, there*. Stumble,
get up, maintain this modest pace, face
skywards.

                High
along the ridge-road fields fizz green, sun
turns, flexing towards spring. Frith
and blaze announce the sudden second beside
our tern —

            two for joy.

Reflection

This poem imagines the experience of sorrow and the re-emergence of joy and gain after a time of loss. Framed by the first two lines of the nursery rhyme 'One For Sorrow', its images are of human resilience learnt from observing natural patterns, but not without awareness of the effort it takes to continue and the sense of alienation that can attend trauma's aftermath. The poem has its lighter tones and solitary grief and sea imagery give way to images of earth, green and spring, as the 'lone turn' opens towards hope.

Felicity Plunkett

Three hares

Sandra Renew

When She goes to work at the facility she wears black. She tallies time using atomic clocks. She catches errant seconds, locks them into leap seconds, and calculates them into leap days.
She regulates, controls, monitors, minds, meddles. No parallel universe, no time travel, no time going slowly, no dragging time, no split seconds.

But, in the darkest sleepless nights, she likes the idea of bringing time to a complete stop.

three hares leap
in the warming moon
beat dry grass
down to a fairy circle
a dance silver as time

Footnote: this is an ekphrastic piece from the Dancing Hares sculpture by Sophie Ryder, 'Annual Spring Courtship'

Reflection

I have selected this tanka prose piece for the *This Gift, This Poem*, that it might inspire a moment of interest, and then joy in the juxtaposition of the ideas. It can happen that, when things are not the best, we sense that time might defeat us. However, just the idea that we might intervene in time can bring a wry, accepting acknowledgement that we cannot.

And still, the joy of the hares leaping in the moonlight can gift us a moment outside our own care of the world.

Sandra Renew

Sweet Peas

Carolyn Rickett

for my parents

'The green shoot will break through the rock …
our tombs of loss will shatter, and there will be a
homecoming. There will. There will. There will.'
—Lewis Packer

Every year your hands wire trellis to the sloping fence
staking out the hope of something more than grey.

Then with a watering can you form a nimbus cloud
and rain on seeds in drought-bound soil.

We wait not knowing when the awkward stalk who keeps
tight-lipped for weeks might have something to say.

And always, every year, the first flower calls us outside
to hear its perfumed mouth finally speaking colour.

Reflection

Some of the earliest memories I have of my parents are our collaborations on shared garden projects. There were the yearly rituals marked and measured by the changing seasons: the training of broad beans and passionfruit vines, gentle indentations made for daffodil and gladioli bulbs, and the careful spacing of poppies and pansies to ensure full flourishing.

The poem 'Sweet Peas' acknowledges not only the reassuring continuity of the natural world, but more significantly is a recognition of familial bonds and the myriad ways in which my mother and father cared for us and created opportunities for our growth.

Along with acknowledging my parents, this poem was first written when Judith Beveridge and I envisioned the *New Leaves* writing group for people experiencing life-threatening illnesses and also serves as a tribute to them. This poem, and the name for our writing group, was inspired by Richard Aldington's poem 'New Love' where his four-line epigram images an almond tree producing new leaves after being damaged by frost. The plant's regenerative capacity metaphorically suggests that while disease may diminish a human body, the human heart continues to seek and produce meaningful connection. The emergent buds also symbolically represent the ways in which creativity may offer something emotionally healing, which is my hope for readers of this anthology.

My mother is now in her 90s. Yesterday, dodging cold winter winds, and in the faithful company of Issy our Cavalier King Charles Spaniel, we finished this year's planting. She gently passed me last year's harvested sweet pea seeds as we moved together between garden rows pressing them into the earth with part water, part sun, part hope and full joy.

Carolyn Rickett

Who, if I cried out, would hear me among the angelic orders?

Rilke

Robyn Rowland

for June and Bronwyne, Aged care home-help

None. But these come, grounded angels,
more useful than the litany of winged
messengers each religion offers.
Always calm, always giving, they wear violet.
Invisible among us, I didn't know them
till exhausted, I cried out for help,
buckling under this burden, this loved parent,
a man, one hundred years of age.

Wings of dragonfly gossamer, frets
of hidden steel, engined by light
as angels are, their inner pulse is compassion,
humour the fluid in their veins.
Gifts are lodged in them we cannot see
revealed slowly over time.
When they come, they rewind his memories
with word games, cards, old albums.

Magic conjurors, they help him
shuffle his stories into newness,
those I have heard a thousand times.
They coax him, where I command,
laugh easily while my smile feels set.
Each muscle in me aches, tendons tighten.
Hands over-used, fingers click a painful rebellion.
I am heart-tired, bone-tired, too weary even to weep.

They tell me everything, all this, is normality.
They teach me how to clear away risk,
equip bedroom, bathroom, to watch
his body, to glove myself into forbearance,
needed to clean up mishaps, how to bandage.
They are fearless of his old skin,
'leaking legs', limbs so full of fluid his cells
weep, as if those fleshy blocks are melting.

Their glance is gentle on us.
I feed on their kindness, the babe in caring I am.
I want to be the good daughter
they tell me I am. I see him slipping.
Sadness swells in me, a reservoir
dammed below the sills of my eyes.
Sometimes when they come,
they make me go and walk the beach.

I collect the broken bones of shells,
twisted fluted spines, white and lovely
in their fleshlessness, glass fragments rolled
a million times smooth, translucent, pearly, bottle-green.
I place them on my window-ledge with fan-shells
the colour of sunset, an empty shark egg. This attention
to amassing the shattered, the crushed on the sands,
is respite from the loss in my father's draining life.

Reflection

When I started caring for my father in December 2018, he was a month off 100 but still playing good lawn bowls, driving, cooking and living independently. His good health had enabled me to travel and to live in Ireland and Turkey with daily Skype chats. He was determined to stay in his home and I to help with this. I never knew how hard that would be, emotionally, physically, mentally. But here we are 16 months later in a routine of strange companionship. He is 101. He is very tired and can't figure out why! I'm very tired and think I'm still sane! This poem was written about June–August 2020. I was calling my Warrigal carers who do his showers 3 times a week my Purple Angels, their uniform colour. Researching angels, I found that every religion has them. But mine are more practical than any of them! I've learned so much and keep learning – to do things I never thought I could. The intimacies of caring for an elderly man are often confronting. Now the team from Warrigal grows as Dad weakens. I am daily moved to gratitude by their kindness, advice and laughter, as well as their care for Dad and myself. This is my thank you.

Robyn Rowland

New Roots, New Beginnings

Patricia M Saar

I hope you like this place and can stay a while.
When you and your companion first came here
We found a sunny spot
Where you could both be seen in all your glory.

Your companion grew broad and tall,
Covered in striking pink
How sad that the sun was too much for you
And you drew back, revealing the skeleton beneath.

You were uprooted, moved to a shadier place,
But your red displace could barely be seen
And you became pale and fragile.
So another place became your home.

Not too much heat,
Not too much wind,
It seemed you were settled at last.
Your deep, red blooms again on show, until –

Elbowing you out of the way
With their insistent search for space and sun –
Came two intruders.
So you moved back to a sheltered place,

But you were thirsty, and started to fade again.
Now a new bed is ready.
Japonica Nova Zembla, here you stand,
Establishing new roots, part of a garden once more.

Like you, I have been uprooted, changed, moved to one side,
Lacking the nourishment I craved, and faltering
When the demands of others became overwhelming.
Now I am looking for just the right place

To put down new roots, a new foundation,
To stand tall with new supports, new ways of seeing.
We will make a new beginning together,
And see if we both can prosper.

Reflection

I wrote this poem when I first joined the *New Leaves* writing group, and it is one of my first poems as I typically wrote prose at that time. I wanted to write about my own experience of transitions in life, and in particular the move from my old house where I had many memories to a new house with future ones to create.

While this poem literally describes the translocation of one of my favourite plants from its old home to its new home, it also explores my own resilience in 'putting down' new roots. I hope that readers of this poem will feel encouraged and strengthened by the possibilities of new beginnings even though our lives experience uncertainties.

Patricia M Saar

Afternoon at La Pietra

Melinda Smith

Someone has silk-stockinged the sun.
Every yellow villa wall is a spread net
of marigold. For afternoons like this,

marble is hewn and placed as an offering;
a creamy glowline flares along a pale brow,
a marvel of cheekbone; a spread palm

cups its blessing of radiance. For afternoons like this,
words like burnish and mellow are required,
are called into being. Words like worship.

Do not say them yet.
Stand a moment in the late gold day.
Look upon the rock, the brick, the carved, the uncarved,

taking their bright, slant benediction. See and stay silent,
see stone itself anointed and caused to speak,
blindingly eloquent with light.

Reflection

Sometimes the moments that shift everything for us happen at unlikely times and in unlikely places. On a street corner, in a forest, in the elevator, under a cloudy sky. For a heartbeat, perhaps a few breaths, we can touch the mystery that lives beneath the surface of the physical world. This poem attempts to capture something like that. By its very nature this is a difficult thing to put into words, and the poem also enacts this struggle. I offer it as a small solace, a smooth stone to hold in the hand against whatever you are facing.

Melinda Smith

The chapel astronomer

Shane Strange

The end of things might be this room of stone orange from the imperfect, coloured glass no bigger than a sheet of newsprint left lying on the wall. One can see hands cut and laid the flagstones rubbed away by centuries of leather clad feet. And I am thinking of my boy and how these one thousand, ten thousand, one hundred thousand pairs of hands and eyes have made this room a living place of generations for me and for him there is something in that—the humility of life. Please. Please. Put eyelets in the sky for his stars.

Reflection

This poem comes from a time when my son was critically ill in a hospital in Barcelona, Spain. Between visiting hours (strictly enforced) I took myself off to nearby places of interest, hoping for distraction of mind and body. One of these places was the Monastery of Pedralbles – a Gothic monastery founded in 1326.

As I entered a small prayer room just off the cloisters, with its worn flagstones, its uneven floors and small, imperfect, orange glass window high in the opposing wall, it came upon me suddenly – a sense of being part of something larger.

I am not a religious person, and even in this most distressing of times, I could not summon a God to pray to. But what came to me was an imagination of generations of human effort and belief that went into the idea of that humble room, the monastery, the church. How many people had been here over the centuries in situations such as mine, or with their own worries and fears? Whose hands built and rebuilt this place? Whose feet had worn down this floor? Perhaps, I thought, *that* might be something to believe in, something in my own secular and cynical way to 'pray' to.

Shane Strange

Butterflies Twice Landed

Patricia Sykes

In the year you cheat death
you argue with portents
and are compelled by butterflies

two in one week alighting
on skin needled and savaged
by chemo drugs, why else

be stunned that your toxic blood
attracts the most beautiful wings
be transformed if you like

(solace is in the signs?)

at worst be baffled
by prognostic high flights:
15% survival might be short

of optimal but Dr Knife
is not your final sleep
you are greedier than ever

for green sunlight, winged
optimism transports you
at least long enough for butterflies

to use you as positive space

Reflection

I've chosen this poem for the way it reflects the healing power of optimism and belief in the life force. You expect butterflies to land on you if you're in a butterfly house but not when walking around at home. I was living on an acre opposite a forest in the Dandenongs at the time and was stunned when two butterflies in the one week landed on my skin. I was definitely not emitting floral odours! I was undergoing 3 months of hourly chemotherapy prior to surgery to remove my stomach and spleen due to cancer. The wonder of them not being repelled by my emaciated and toxic body is still with me 13 years later.

Patricia Sykes

Don't say anything

Andrew Taylor

Don't say anything –
I can see in your eyes
what you dare not say
what you mustn't say
that would crack the silence that binds us

*

I can see in that photo
the pain in your eyes
not my pain that you're watching
but the pain within you
in your watching

*

My pain will end
if it must
yours will live in the silence
the clarity
of an empty bed

*

No – that's eighteen years past
and we need say
nothing –
mere words are speechless
when I read the eloquence

of your eyes

Reflection

When I was seriously ill with cancer almost twenty years ago my wife's silent strength helped me more than any words could to persevere and eventually fully recover. I have a photo of her taken then showing her distress. Because she gave her strength also to me, I was able to try to help her too in that difficult time. That's what the poem tries to express. Today that bond doesn't need to be put into words, except perhaps in a poem.

Andrew Taylor

Solace

Gillian Telford

(i)
Out of rhythm
and far from my own quiet spaces,
I discover the fountain:
          its voices lap my thoughts —
          subdue the inner sea.

Around me, wisteria writhes
and reaches out
as if to hide its knotted veins:
          from these depths a bird pipes out
with small, defiant notes.

Box-hedged, I breathe the humus deep,
          catch the yellow leaf
that drifts across my hand
and let the fountain's flow
re-set my metronome.

(ii)
Day after day of wind and rain —
          autumn's load spins down
to pile in saffron drifts.

Now the wisteria's sap has dried
and last week's potent wands
hang down in listless claws.

But the bird still calls
from its sheltered perch;
the sun can penetrate the shade

while from my hidden seat
I hear the fountain lions
pour out their endless balm.

Reflection

This poem arose during a time when one of my young grandchildren was extremely ill and I moved interstate for several months to help. As many women experience, there are times when we're needed as mothers and grandmothers, yet still have competing demands as daughters of elderly parents. Juggling priorities and emotions was fraught, particularly being so far from the refuge and support of my own home base.

One day, with a spare half hour, I called in to a large, city park and sat in a secluded corner, almost hidden from others, but able to watch and listen. This spot became my special quiet place, somewhere I could go to meditate, to draw breath and gather myself together again. I found comfort too in the changing seasons and the hope shown in nature's renewal.

Whether we are the carer, or the ones being cared for, we all need a place where we can nurture ourselves. And even when the body is weak or confined, we can close our eyes and visit the parks and fountains of the mind.

Gillian Telford

Writing on Electrons

Richard Kelly Tipping

imagine silence and   solitude firm as bread.
imagine hunger cutting   first slice, first breath.
imagine silence, answering   each syllable back.
imagine, alone, around,   yourself the only sound.

all creatures are aware.   intense existences
the crumbling rock escapes   ideas of time
and change   a single cell has planets and suns -
all life emitting light   into interstellar dreaming.

writing on electrons, entering the body of the immortals
a shadow of the actual   midnight on the dot, in heaven
living by luck alone   the same things will still exist.
we'd gladly be gods   but it would spoil the game.

animals made people: never forget that.   the Earth
was helpless against sheer will   and a good idea.
cosmologies entwined: so eternity *is* in love with
the productions of time!   now you know everything.

the snake bites its tail,   the wheel invents the road.
three words across the path: *now is forever*
finding that little place inside   where all the stars
come out -   there is another world, and it is this one.

intuition thickens into presence: the senses
of animals, sniffing   and listening in the dark.
life shrinks from infinity - beyond light no matter.
your ego pops   under lack of pressure.

is it into aeons   of nothingness we go
where time never starts   or float forever, bliss
in some brimming   immeasurable flow   and our
hearts   these wildest flowers   forget desire?

language binds us with invisible threads to the
translucent body of our illusions.   how can
a drop of water ever be saved from drying up?
the Buddha replied: by throwing it into the sea.

in the freshly   unfolded archives   of our sleep
all loves undone   in threads   weaving slowly
Sun's dream   a golden warmth
covers us with morning

Reflection

'Writing on Electrons' grew from my design for a nine-part sculpture. I needed four-line poems with lines of roughly even length, to have engraved by sand-blasting into nine large basalts crystals which weigh several hundred kilograms apiece. This poem-sculpture embodies the lines within solid natural forms, engaging through poetry with philosophy, science and linguistics in the context of a public space.

Voice is the first state of poetry. Poetry lives and breathes through its song. Line-breaks encourage the reader to SAY the poem, not just skim it by quick reading, so that words have resonance in their spoken sound. The individual stones embody poetic language which can be remembered and passed on.

I looked through my published and unpublished poems seeking intensity, a lightly held seriousness, and self-contained structure. These are my 'arguments with time' placed in a wide circle. The nine four-line sections are each poems rather than stanzas as they may be read in any order. The short independent pieces work independently but gain from each other as a sequence.

Readers of William Blake will recognise from his Proverbs of Hell: 'Eternity is in love with the productions of time'. The other line in Writing on Electrons which floats as a meme is: 'There is another world, and it is this one'. This comes from deep in the intertwining legacies of poets quoting one another and cannot be reliably attributed to any one author.

The sculpture itself is yet to find a permanent home, but a second version of one stone ('in the freshly / unfolded archives / of our sleep …') was made and is now in the gardens of Lake Macquarie's Museum of Art and Culture in New South Wales.

Richard Kelly Tipping

A Short Story of Flying

Mark Tredinnick

After Alice Oswald

IT IS the story of the calling bird:
    A secret freely shared but rarely heard.

It's flying spooled, and sky distilled and swilled,
    Like waking, across the dawn, the lawn, the field

Of maize, the forest in the afternoon.
    It is the spinning world, its waxing moon;

A tide that turns in things, the way a river
    Springs from rock, the shock of hope, the shiver

That thrills inside the thought of rested wings:
    The way a coiled mind now calms—and springs

Again into the flight it knew before
    It fouled its lines along a loreless shore.

It is the lyric of the patient earth
    That wants the sky to be its second birth.

If freedom is the hardest edge to hold,
    This is how it's held—unbought, unsold.

This morning it's the song two spinebills climb
    Into the rigging of midwinter's rhyme

That's undressed every garden tree and woken
    Me to days like doors that want to open.

Chords that want to cry grief down, they've flown,
  As one must let the past, before I've grown

Some legs and found the heart to rise and score
  Their music on this page as if it were

My own. And overnight it was the owls,
  Like books of wanton hours, the crooning fowls

That mistake every midnight for the dawn.
  Let their eternal error be my own

Diurnal trick. A moral overheard:
  The breaking story of the calling bird.

Note: This poem takes its shape and rhyme and rhythm scheme from Alice Oswald's 'A Short Story of Falling,' which, rising, it answers.

Reflection

LIFE is a gift; I give it back in poetry. This is how it has long felt to me.

'A Short Story of Flying' feels like it was given to me, rather than written by me. I wrote it in response to a poem by Alice Oswald, 'A Short Story of Falling,' a poem ostensibly about rain and sorrow. I wrote mine in the same form—heroic couplets (rhyming couplets, each line an iambic pentameter). But whereas hers falls, as life sometimes does, as the heart sometimes does, mine flies, as a life also sometimes does, even when it feels too heavy to take off. If the poem, in its imagery and playfulness with sound and sense, and in its rhythms, helps you take flight again after sorrow or defeat or illness, it will have worked. And you have Alice Oswald to thank for that.

In two other ways, though 'A Short Story' is a poem of gifts. 1.Birdsong (both the spinebills and the rooster the poem alludes to) inspired it, as much as Oswald's poem, and the poem hopes that all who read it remain open to the inspiration of the more than merely human world. 2. Two lines in the poem I have carried with me for years, and I was glad to finally find them a home—'A secret freely shared but rarely heard,' which arose from a conversation with Kim Stafford once about how few people seem to notice the birds, and 'If freedom is the hardest edge to hold...,' a thought I live by. We long, all of us, to be and live and stay free, while also belonging and staying safe. Poetry is a way to reconcile those two contradictory desires. It models a way we might live both ways at once.

Mark Tredinnick

Grace

Todd Turner

There was something in the rain, in the way it fell.
Something in the way of the birds. And in
the way of the river. Something in the way it fell.
Something about how the river rose, and
about the stillness of the birds on the banks
in the rain
and about the way the air made it feel possible
to forgive –
and be forgiven.

Reflection

The writing of 'Grace' was one of those rare moments where the poem seemed to arrive as if out of nowhere, and probably because it was at a time in my life where I needed poetry more than ever. That way of writing very rarely happens for me. In many ways it was a gift and a revelation.

Todd Turner

Along Gertrude Street

Chris Wallace-Crabbe

As the slow going smears purple
over lacklustre lanes and walls
an odd stray cat slips wantonly under
somebody's garage door,
and all that
bluestone cableway is feeling a tad more
eloquent for the time as it were being,
for the leaden time solidified,

so it ravels out that
everything is going, or coming,
to turn out more or less OK
as you round the next corner
where tram slogan and icy-pole wrapper
measure the mystery of our days,
north, south, a hundred mildly tragic ways

that are the case itself, blurry, beneficent
on at least this Biblical evening
at the nerves' brushed end.

Remembering how the lean Austrian warned
that we weren't put on earth to
have a good time at all,

you get to light up, steadily
viewing colour-change on stacks or walls
and the orange clouds fading into a fishy grey.

Reflection

For me, Gertrude Street boasts various identities, mixed complexions. When I was a very young man, it was the site, or lair of many public exams we had to sit at the year's end. It had furniture stores, which we didn't need yet, and a couple of art galleries. Fitzroy could mean mere poverty, but it did have a League football team. And my mother had grown up there, quite demurely. Its name was Norman and genteel. It was also close to Melbourne University, my stamping ground.

For years I have studied, then taught or done my research at this inner-urban university that perches on a large city. Hence Gertrude Street is physically coloured by years and seasons, industry and academic studies.

Chris Wallace-Crabbe

Floating Backwards

Julie Watts

they walk bent as
bows through the dunes

feet shuffling through
memory of sand

heads bowed to the wind & gull
huddle together on the sloped
white ship

the waking in their toes
intent on the shoreline.

here they disrobe
drop years from their bodies
with each discarding

the sagging cardigan
crumpled skirt & trouser

arise from the dumping
like new birds.

feet edge into liminal
saltwater slush sending shocks

wind picks up their hair
throws it behind them

& they face the sea
all their lined histories

enter their past
water transforming skin

lengthening backbones
flooding sinus   infusing muscle.

there are children in Watermans Bay
floating backwards

rotating   sinking
under the slow curl
of wave

laughing   splashing
drifting in the thermals.

later   a couple   bent as
bows will shuffle themselves
back to the Boardwalk

cardigans   undone
sandals in fists
hair   full of sand.

Reflection

Our bodies age but a part of us remains ageless and open to joy and wonder and this part is rediscovered whenever we play. One day at the beach I watched an old couple, bent and stiff, shuffling down the dunes to have a swim together. They discarded their old clothes, entered the water, and began to float backwards into another version of themselves. The transformative power of the ocean reconnected the old couple with their child within, awakened muscle memory and they remembered how to play: splashing, laughing and spinning. They returned up the beach in their old clothes, still bent and stiff, but they remained transformed and free, the child was still there, revitalised – hair full of sand. My hope for the reader is that they vicariously experience the couple's joy of play, freedom and the rediscovered child and maybe be inspired to reconnect with their own child from time to time, through nature and play, and experience the same joy and freedom.

Julie Watts

Da capo

Jen Webb

When the air is soft, and the sun sits perfectly on the horizon, and the neighbour's boy opens his window so the voice of his cello washes against the fence. When the magpies sing for their supper, and the marigolds store the light of the sun against the night hours. Inside the house right now it's all prowling, and voices that crack and fall. Inside is all shake and shudder, and you need to sign that form and you realise you've bought only purple garlic, not white, and the cat has trapped herself in the cupboard again, and no one has emptied the bin. Breathe. It's easily fixed. You pass out drinks, and comfort the cat, and calm comes in with the evening light, and the sun sets, perfectly, and night curls itself around the house.

Reflection

I have a tendency to write about the grimmer side of life, and need to remind myself, when it comes to editing my poems, that sorrow is not more lyrical than joy. This poem began its life thinking about the chaos and stress in family homes I have known, but when I spent time reflecting on the images that were its genesis, what came to mind was the softness of evening light; the busy goings-on among the more-than-human beings among whom we live (the trees; the birds; the flowers); and about what a remarkable privilege it is to be part of a safe and fundamentally community-minded suburb. I named it 'da capo', which is the musical instruction to start again from the beginning – to repeat a passage; and hoped in this naming to remind myself that we are always starting afresh, each day; repeating our everyday actions and activities; and experiencing as though for the first time all the small everyday beauties that are threaded through our environments.

Jen Webb

Leaning Backwards with Great-Aunt Natalie

Annamaria Weldon

She clutches me for support and with her cane points
at the Marri tree strung with Clematis, climbing
tendrils in tight spirals, blossoms like white tutus.

Is she remembering her students, tender-limbed
sapling ballerinas, rounded arms slightly raised
heels together, toes turned out in first position?

On ancient Red Gums, early Spring unfurls new leaves
lustrous, tips tinged with a youthful blush. The light wind
sways their thin stems, bending them away from the stalks.

My Russian aunt has started humming *Les Etudes*
her head tilting to the rhythm as if she were
in her studio again. In its mirrors I see

her flowing chiffon scarf draped from neck to flexed wrist.
She's keeping tempo with one jewelled hand outstretched
as if to steady the supple bodies, spines bent

backwards from the barre which small hands clasp for guidance.
Thin wrists strain as standing tall again each dancer
lifts one leg high, finds balance leaning on old wood.

Reflection

My first awareness that charisma emanates from an inner well and has nothing to do with one's age dawned when I studied ballet in Malta with my great-aunt Princess Natalie Poutiatine, born in St Petersburg in 1904, who died in Malta in 1984. That was the very year I came to Australia from Malta, so I never saw her again, she never visited us here. But like an immortal, she left an indelible impression. This poem came with her spirit during a walk in the bush while *Clematis pubescens* was in flower. The bush works that way on me sometimes. Already a ballerina, Natalie fled her Russian birthland in April 1919, following the uprising of the Bolsheviks and the assassination of Tsar Nicholas II in 1917. Together with her mother Princess Olga, Natalie arrived in Malta in April 1919 and remained there until 1921, when she continued with her ballet studies in Paris. In 1927 she returned to Malta following her marriage to my Great-Uncle Edgar Tabone. I attended her Studio in Malta first as a schoolgirl, later as a mature student, when Natalie was in her eighties, *still* an icon of resilience, passion and elegance.

Further biographical details: https://poutiatineandtheartofballet.wordpress.com/princess-natalie-poutiatine/

Annamaria Weldon

On World Heart Day

Jane Williams

I notice your scars more than usual –
life-saving stuck zippers.
I want to plant kisses
like votives along each one:
along the delicate ribbon of light
between your extroverted nipples,
along the scythe shaped slash
de-freckling your right calf.
Hospital flowers bloomed, petals fell
in the sterile-fresh air that day.
I wove endearments like chainmail
across the terrible divide
as miracle drugs fought to save you,
leaving demons in their wake.
Somewhere in your addled brain
a small piece of trust remained
and you gave it to me –
love's indefatigable radar homing in.
That first night home we read
Postoperative Delirium over beer
and ice cream the way we once
read *The Heart is a Lonely Hunter.*
With no more to wish for we fell asleep
to the tick of your tin man heart.
But they cracked open your breast bone
and I cannot think too long on this.
The pressure it took. The precision.
The stillness of your heart and lungs.
The machine that breathed for you.
The one that brightened your blood.

And the tunnel, that anecdotal tunnel
you say you never saw coming
returning you to me like fortune,
my light-scarred Lazarus love.

Reflection

For me poetry is the language of the soul. It enables me to communicate ideas and experiences in ways that everyday conversation can't always accommodate.

In 2011 my partner underwent difficult and lengthy heart surgery. While the operation was a success, it was an anxious and painful time for both of us. He jokes now about belonging to the 'zipper club', recognizing the tell-tale scar rising up from the open-necked shirts of other men. And we have grown accustomed to the alien sound of his mechanical valve. But the transience and tenderness of life sits with us a little differently now. Just below the surface.

'On World Heart Day' was a tough poem to write but it has been an important one for us to read as a reminder to honour our days together and the memories we make. I hope others find it similarly meaningful.

Jane Williams

Maybe the Moon

Kimberly Williams

What dwells beyond
gratitude? The sun
touching fire to the earth's
rim, the day moon, three-

quarters full on the rise,
the metamorphosis searing

citrine, peridot, lapis lazuli
to decorate fingers and necks.

Maybe the cloud cradling dusk.
Maybe the water following its trail

of rocks like a hound dog following
a scent. Maybe the sliver of moon
hanging cockeyed in the sky.
Maybe. Whatever lies
beyond is nothing. We can touch.

Reflection

This poem comes from that feeling that arrives now and again which extends beyond gratitude -- just that rare moment that sneaks up, perhaps whilst I'm staring at the stars or standing at the edge of the ocean, or even on a mid-week evening watching the sun slip behind the hills at the edge of my suburb. It's that moment where everything feels right because the world is just so immense, and our human smallness in it for once works to our advantage. Part of that feeling, I think, comes from being reminded that life is happening at a large geological, universal level. Whilst we go about our individual human lives, the earth revolves around the sun; the moon has its way with the tides, and geo-chemical reactions happen deep within the earth creating precious stones. I wrote this poem to contemplate and pay tribute to that vastness and to those moments of marvel. For me those are the moments that offer hope, and something I wish to share through this poem.

Kimberly Williams

With Gratitude

In her moving interview with Krista Tippett for the *On Being* podcast, beloved poet Mary Oliver offers a reflection on the process of writing and sharing poetry:

> It is a convivial and kind of — it's very old. It's very sacred. It wishes for a community. It's a community ritual, certainly. And that's why, when you write a poem, you write it for anybody and everybody. And you have to be ready to do that out of your single self. It's a giving. It's always — it's a gift. It's a gift to yourself but it's a gift to anybody who has a hunger for it.[5]

Our anthology has at its heart this idea of community, and poetry itself being a gift that is shared and received. Over the years I have had the privilege of researching in the field of medical humanities and working in healthcare chaplaincy and have seen the ways in which poetry can provide comfort and solace to people experiencing distress and who may be feeling isolated. The vision for this anthology continues to build on the *New Leaves* project where writing and reading poetry are seen as ways of promoting wellbeing through the largesse of poets contributing their work and promoting solidarity through sharing the written word.

The kindness of poets gifting their work to readers of *This Gift, This Poem* anthology means the original aspiration of wanting patients and families waiting in liminal hospital spaces, or residents living in aged care settings, to feel they are not alone — and to hold a tangible book which may be returned to in times of distress and loneliness — is now a reality.

---

5 Tippet, Krista, host. 'Mary Oliver listening to the world.' On being with Krista Tippet, 5 February 2018, https://onbeing.org/programs/mary-oliver-listening-to-the-world/

Thank you to each poet who thoughtfully contributed something they hoped would nourish the reader and wrote a reflection to personalise their gift.

And abiding thanks to Judith Beveridge for her mentorship and generous championing of poetry projects with heart, Jean Kent for the early conversations about why this project matters so much and for her tireless editorial work and generosity of spirit, Dr David Musgrave for his unflagging commitment to writing, promoting and publishing poetry, and Professor Jen Webb for her editorial collaboration and vision for the ways in which poetry may support human beings in times of crisis.

I am deeply grateful for the ongoing support from Avondale University's leaders Professor Kevin Petrie and Professor Kerri-Lee Krause and their ethic of care in valuing initiatives which contribute to the wellbeing of communities. We are indebted to—and are cheered on by— the enthusiastic encouragement of Associate Professor Darren Morton, Director of the Lifestyle Medicine and Health Research Centre, who provided funding for this project, and acknowledge too The Centre for Advancement of the Scholarship of Teaching and Learning (CASTL) at Avondale University who also contributed sponsorship for this anthology. I wish to also express gratitude for Margaret House and her work on manuscript preparation and Design & Prosper for the artistic cover design.

And to Professor Brett Mitchell and colleagues from Avondale University, The University of Sydney, The University of Newcastle, University of Technology Sydney, and the University of Canberra who over many years have been and remain great encouragers of wellbeing poetry projects— thank you. Pr Stenoy Stephenson and members of the Spiritual Care Services team and staff at Sydney Adventist Hospital (The SAN), thank you for your inspiring commitment to patients and their families. Your generous presence continues to demonstrate the ways in which we can serve others with engaged compassion.

Special thanks to Althea Halliday, Professor Jane Fernandez,

Dr Robyn Priestley, Dr Drene Somasundrum, Professor Paul Race, Professor Daniel Reynaud, Lynnette Lounsbury, Associate Professor Sue Joseph, Associate Professor Peter Kilgour, Professor Maria Northcote, Professor Ray Roennfeldt, Professor Tony Williams, Tony Martin, Andy Collis, Richard Morris, Donna Pinter, Carie Browning, the New Leaves writing group, Dr Bronwyn Steele, Daniel Ionita, Stuart and Cherie Tipple, Sue Dawson, Pippa Lee, Ann Campbell, Emma Kalaf, Brenton Stacey, Bruna Tawake, Professor Jill Gordon, Professor William Christie, Dr Victoria Burrows, Dr Bernadette Brennan, Dr Noel Rowe and Associate Professor Rebecca Johinke who have each contributed significantly to the ways in which literature is valued, and more broadly how the Humanities can enhance and expand a moral purpose. As Mary Oliver reminds us in *A Poetry Handbook*: 'Poetry is a life-cherishing force. For poems are not words, after all, but fires for the cold, ropes let down to the lost, something as necessary as bread in the pockets of the hungry.'[6]

Associate Professor Carolyn Rickett

---

6 Oliver, Mary. *A Poetry Handbook*. Harcourt Brace & Co, 1994, 122.

Biographical Notes

MAGDALENA BALL is a novelist, poet, reviewer and interviewer, and is the Managing Editor of Compulsive Reader. She has been widely published in literary journals, anthologies, and online, and is the author of several published books of poetry and fiction, including, most recently *Unreliable Narratives* (Girls on Key Press, 2019). A new book titled *Density of Compact Bone* is forthcoming from Ginninderra Press in late 2021.

JUDITH BEVERIDGE lives in Sydney, Australia. She has published seven volumes of poetry and has edited or co-edited a number of anthologies including *Contemporary Australian Poetry*, (Puncher & Wattmann, 2016). She was poetry editor for *Meanjin* from 2005-2016. Her work has been studied in schools and universities and translated into many languages. Her latest volume *Sun Music: New and Selected Poems* (Giramondo, 2018), won the Prime Minister's Poetry Prize in 2019.

PETER BOYLE is a Sydney-based poet and translator of poetry. He has nine books of poetry published and eight books as a translator. His most recent collection is *Notes Towards the Dreambook of Endings* (Vagabond Press, 2021). In 2020 his book *Enfolded in the Wings of a Great Darkness* won the New South Wales Premier's Award for Poetry.

LISA BROCKWELL was born and raised in Sydney and spent a large chunk of her early adult life in London. She now lives in Edinburgh and in Byron Bay. Her poems have been published in *The Spectator*, *The Canberra Times*, *The Weekend Australian*, *Meanjin* and *Best Australian Poems*. Her first book, *Earth Girls* (Pitt Street Poetry) was commended in the Anne Elder Award. *The Round Ring* is forthcoming in 2021.

ANDREW BURKE is a well-established WA writer, with 14 poetry collections published, many short stories and countless book reviews. He had two careers—one in advertising, the other in academia. Now he is retired but still writing. Current title *New and Selected*. Available <ralph.wessman@walleahpress.com.au>

WILLIAM CHRISTIE is Emeritus Professor at the Australian National University (having recently retired as Head of its Humanities Research Centre), Director of the Australasian Consortium of Humanities Research Centres, and a Fellow of the Australian Academy of the Humanities. He is the author of literary biographies of Samuel Taylor Coleridge (which won the NSW Premier's Biennial Prize for Literary Scholarship in 2008) and of Dylan Thomas, as well as of the award-winning play for voices, *Under Mulga Wood*, broadcast and recorded by the ABC.

JOSEPHINE CLARKE has had poetry and short stories published in Australian journals including *Westerly, Cordite* and *Southerly*. Her work was featured in the *ABR*'s States of Poetry WA, Series 2. Her first collection of poetry, *Recipe for Risotto*, was published by UWA Press in July 2020.

KERRYN COOMBS-VALEONTIS is an Ecotherapist, and Ecoart therapist, who is inspired by her connection to Nature. She will launch her first collection of poetry (*in parenthesis*) in August 2021, during International Poetry Month. She collates the Ecopoesis online annual Zine. The reading and writing of poetry is a necessary, and constant survival for her soul.

JUDITH NANGALA CRISPIN is a visual artist and poet of Bpangerang/GunaiKurnai descent. She has published two collections of poetry, *The Myrrh-Bearers* (Sydney: Puncher & Wattmann, 2015), and *The Lumen Seed* (New York: Daylight

Books, 2017). Her illustrated verse novel, *The Dingo's Noctuary*, will be published in 2021. Judith is the current poetry editor of *The Canberra Times*.

MTC CRONIN has published over twenty books (poetry, prose poems and essays), a number of which have appeared in translation.

JAN DEAN's most recent collection, *Intermittent Angels*, was published by Girls on Key in 2020. Her pocketbook *Paint Peels, Graffiti Sings*, (Flying Island Books, Macau, 2014) in English and Mandarin, spans varied poetic forms. *With One Brush*, an art related poetry collection, published by Interactive Publications in 2007, was the Winner of their Best First Book Award and was also short-listed for the Mary Gilmore Award, 2008.

ROSS DONLON has published five collections of poetry, the most recent being *For the Record* (Recent Work Press). Published in numerous journals and anthologies, he has read his poems in festivals both in Australia and Europe. His sequence, 'The Blue Dressing Gown', was a feature on Radio National, ABC.

LUCY DOUGAN's books include *Memory Shell* (5 Islands Press), *White Clay* (Giramondo), *Meanderthals* (Web del Sol) and *The Guardians* (Giramondo) which won the Western Australian Premier's Book Award for poetry. With Tim Dolin, she is co-editor of *The Collected Poems of Fay Zwicky* (UWAP, 2017).

ALI COBBY ECKERMANN's first collection *little bit long time* was written in the desert and launched her literary career in 2009. Her works have been published in various languages, and she has travelled widely to showcase Aboriginal poetry overseas.

STEPHEN EDGAR is the author of eleven collections of poetry, most recently *The Strangest Place: New and Selected Poems* in

2020. His previous three books, *Eldershaw*, *Exhibits of the Sun* and *Transparencies*, were all shortlisted for the Prime Minister's Literary Awards. He received the Philip Hodgins Memorial Medal in 2006 and the Colin Roderick Award in 2014. He lives in Sydney.

ROBERT EDMONDS is a poet, psychologist and clown doctor whose work has appeared in many publications. In 2016 he was longlisted for The University of Canberra Vice Chancellor's International Poetry Prize. In 2020 he won third prize in the $25,000 Newcastle Poetry Prize. His first poetry collection *Gravity Doesn't Always Work* was published by Flying Island Books in 2021.

THEODORE ELL is a writer, translator and editor who lives in Canberra. Born in Sydney, he has also lived in Italy and Lebanon. His poetry has appeared in several newspapers and anthologies in Australia and overseas.

BROOK EMERY has published five books of poetry, the most recent being *have been and are* (Gloria SMH, 2016). He has won the Judith Wright Calanthe Prize at the Queensland Premier's Literary Awards and been short-listed three times for the Kenneth Slessor Prize at the NSW Premier's Literary Awards.

LUKE FISCHER is a poet and philosopher. His various books include the poetry collections *A Personal History of Vision* (UWAP, 2017) and *Paths of Flight* (Black Pepper, 2013) and the monograph *The Poet as Phenomenologist: Rilke and the New Poems (Bloomsbury, 2015)*. He holds a PhD in philosophy and is an honorary associate of the University of Sydney. For more information visit: www.lukefischerauthor.com

JOHN FOULCHER has published poetry in magazines and newspapers throughout Australia for over thirty-five years. His poetry has been widely anthologised and he has published twelve volumes of poetry, the most recent being *Dancing with Stephen Hawking* (Pitt Street Poetry 2021). He lives in Reidsdale in NSW.

KATHRYN FRY has poems in *Antipodes* (2016, 2019), *Cordite Poetry Review* (2016), *Not Very Quiet* (2017-2020 incl.), *Westerly* (2019, 2020) and *Science Write Now* (2020). In 2020, her poem 'About the Centre, Even Now' won the Alice Sinclair Poetry Prize, and she was longlisted for the ACU Prize for Poetry. Her first collection is *Green Point Bearings* (Ginninderra Press, 2018) and her second *The Earth Will Outshine Us*, will be published in 2021, also by Ginninderra Press.

ALTHEA HALLIDAY spent the last part of her English teaching career at Barker College in Sydney. It was here that her heart became entwined in Tim Winton's novel, *Cloudstreet*, a text that she taught for fifteen consecutive years. Now as she composes her memoirs, she still finds herself in that deep 'winy country' of words that never lose their colour.

JENNIFER HARRISON has published eight poetry collections, most recently *Anywhy* (Black Pepper 2018). She manages The Dax Poetry Collection housed at The Dax Centre, University of Melbourne, and co-judges the annual Ann Morgan Prize for the Australian Association for Infant Mental Health. She is currently secretary of the World Psychiatry Association's Section for Art and Psychiatry and in 2012 was awarded the Christopher Brennan Award for sustained contribution to Australian poetry.

DENNIS HASKELL is the author of 9 collections of poetry, the most recent *And Yet...* (WA Poets Publishing, 2020) and the related volume, *Ahead of Us* (Fremantle Press, 2016). He is a Member of the Order of Australia for 'services to literature, particularly poetry, to education and to intercultural understanding'. His website is dennishaskell.com.au

GAIL HENNESSY has been published widely in newspapers, literary supplements, journals and anthologies. Her poetry has won a number of local and national prizes. Her published work includes *Witnessing* (self-published, 2010), *Written on Water* (Flying Island Books, 2017) and *The M Word* (Girls on Key, 2019).

PAUL HETHERINGTON is a distinguished Australian poet who has published 15 full-length books of poetry and prose poetry. He is Professor of Writing in the Faculty of Arts and Design at the University of Canberra, head of the International Poetry Studies Institute (IPSI) and joint founding editor of the journal *Axon: Creative Explorations*.

DANIEL IONITA – born in Bucharest, Romania, teaches Organisational Improvement at the University of Technology Sydney. Published works include *Testament – 400 Years of Romanian Poetry* – a collection of Romanian poetry in English (volume which received the 'Gaudeamus International Bookfair – Bucharest 2019' Prize for Translation), *The Bessarabia of My Soul* – a representation, also in English, of poets from the Republic of Moldova, for which Daniel was awarded the Poetry Prize by the *Literature & Art* magazine in that country. Some of his own poetry volumes are *Hanging Between the Stars, ContraDiction, The Island of Words from Home, Short Bursts of Eternity*. Daniel is the current president of the Australian-Romanian Academy for Culture.

IVY IRELAND is the author of *Incidental Complications* (2007), *Porch Light* (2015) and *The Owl Inside* (2020). Ivy's divergent career paths have included bookstore owner, magician's assistant, musician, cabaret performer, writer, tutor in Creative Writing and academic. Ivy's literary awards include the Australian Young Poet Fellowship, the Harri Jones Memorial Prize, the Thunderbolt Prize, the Newcastle Poetry Prize local award, and she was the runner-up in the UC International Poetry Prize. Ivy completed her Ph.D. in Creative Writing at the University of Newcastle and her poetry, essays and reviews have been widely published in journals and anthologies.

LINDA IRELAND spent 35 years teaching English and Drama in Hunter high schools during which time she received a National Teaching Award. For five years she has been a mentor for ModPO, an international online course in Modern American Poetry run out of the University of Pennsylvania. She is a member of Lake Macquarie's Blue Room Poets and helped establish Poetry At The Lake Mac Pub. Linda's work has appeared in several anthologies, including *Now You Shall Know* (Newcastle Poetry Prize 2013).

ANDY JACKSON's *Music Our Bodies Can't Hold* was shortlisted for the 2020 John Bray Poetry Award. He has co-edited disability-themed issues of the literary journals *Southerly* and *Australian Poetry Journal*, and his new collection of poems, *Human Looking*, is forthcoming in 2021.

JUDY JOHNSON has published five full-length poetry collections and several chapbooks. She has won significant national prizes for her work. Her verse novel *Jack* won the Victorian Premier's Award for poetry and was on both the Sydney and Melbourne University syllabus.

SUE JOSEPH (PhD) has been a journalist for more than forty years. She began working as an academic at the University of Technology Sydney in 1997. As a Senior Lecturer, she taught in journalism and creative writing, particularly creative non-fiction writing. Now as Associate Professor, she holds an Adjunct position at Avondale University, is a Senior Research Fellow at the University of South Australia, and is a doctoral supervisor at the University of Sydney and Central Queensland University. Her fourth book, *Behind the Text: Candid conversations with Australian creative nonfiction writers*, was released in 2016. She co-edited two texts on profile writing: *Profile Pieces: Journalism and the Human Interest Bias* (Routledge 2016) and *The Profiling Handbook* (Abramis Academic Publishing 2015); and two texts on memoir writing: *Mediating Memory: Tracing the Limits of Memoir* (Routledge 2018) and *Still There: memoirs of Trauma, Illness and Loss* (Routledge 2019). She also co-edited in 2019 *Sex and Journalism: Critical, Global Perspectives*, (Bite-sized Books). She is Joint Editor of *Ethical Space: The International Journal of Communication Ethics.*

CHRISTOPHER (KIT) KELEN is a poet and painter, resident in the Myall Lakes of NSW. Published widely since the seventies, he has a dozen full length collections in English as well as translated books of poetry in Chinese, Portuguese, French, Italian, Spanish, Indonesian, Swedish, Norwegian and Filipino. His latest volume of poetry in English is *Poor Man's Coat – Hardanger Poems*, published by UWAP in 2018. His next volume *a book of mother* is forthcoming from Puncher & Wattmann. You can keep up to date with Kit on *the daily kit –* https://thedailykitkelen.blogspot.com/

JEAN KENT grew up in rural Queensland and now lives at Lake Macquarie, NSW. Eight books of her poetry have been published: the most recent are *The Hour of Silvered Mullet* (Pitt Street Poetry, 2015) and *Paris in my Pocket* (PSP, 2016). Her collection *Verandahs* won the Anne Elder Prize and the Dame Mary Gilmore Award; *The Satin Bowerbird* was awarded the Wesley Michel Wright Prize. Jean has also worked as an educational psychologist, counsellor in TAFE colleges and teacher of creative writing. Her website is jeankent.net.au

ANDY KISSANE lives in Sydney and writes poetry and fiction. He was joint winner of ABR's 2019 Peter Porter Prize for Poetry. *Radiance* was shortlisted for the Victorian and Western Australian Premier's Prizes and the Adelaide Festival Awards. His latest book is *The Tomb of the Unknown Artist.* www.andykissane.com

SHARI KOCHER is an award-winning poet, remedial therapist and scholar whose work has been featured in literary journals in Australia and elsewhere spanning more than three decades. She is the author of *The Non-Sequitur of Snow* (Puncher & Wattmann 2015), *Foxstruck and Other Collisions* (Puncher & Wattmann, 2021) and *Sonqoqui: a Threnody*, which is currently in translation under the auspices of the *The Peter Steele Poetry Prize* (2020). She holds MA and Doctorate degrees from Melbourne University, where she sometimes works as a sessional teaching associate and postgraduate supervisor in the Creative Writing program.

RICHARD LANDER was born in the Riverina, educated at the University of Sydney and is now retired. He commenced writing poetry as a form of therapy after being diagnosed with prostate cancer in 2007. Some of Richard's earlier poetry has been published in other Puncher & Wattmann anthologies including *All These Presences* (2016), *Wording the World* (2010), *Here Not There* (2012), *A Way of Happening* (2014) and *On First Looking* (2018) and *The New Leaves Anthology* (2008) published by Darlington Press. He is a member of the New Leaves writing group.

MARTIN LANGFORD has published seven books of poetry – most recently *Eardrum* (Puncher and Wattmann, 2020), a book of poems about music. He was co-editor (with J. Beveridge, J. Johnson and D. Musgrave) of *Contemporary Australian Poetry* (P&W, 2016). He is the poetry reviewer for *Meanjin*.

ANDREW LANSDOWN is a widely published and award-winning Australian writer whose works include 3 novels, 2 short story collections, 2 children's poetry collections, 2 photography-and-poetry collections and 15 poetry collections. His most recent books are: *Distillations of Different Lands* (Sunline Press, Western Australia, 2018); *Kyoto Momiji Tanka: Poems and Photographs of Japan in Autumn* (Rhiza Press, Queensland, 2019); and *Abundance: New and Selected Poems* (Wipf & Stock/ Cascade Books, Oregon, 2020). His website is: www.andrewlansdown.com

PENELOPE LAYLAND is an award-winning Canberra poet and a former journalist and speechwriter. Her most recent book is *Nigh* (Recent Work Press 2020).

LYNNETTE LOUNSBURY is a writer, filmmaker and educator who lives in Sydney, Australia. She is the author of two novels (*Afterworld, We Ate the Road like Vultures*) and has published poetry in several anthologies including *Love in the Time of Corona: Notes from a Pandemic* (2020), *A Way of Happening* (2014) and *Here Not There* (2012).

WIN LUBEN is a retired nurse who lives in Sydney and has a keen interest in learning about other cultures and exploring new languages. She is a member of the *New Leaves* writing group.

GREG McLAREN is a poet, teacher and sometime critic who lives on Darug and Gandangara country in the lower Blue Mountains. He has been anthologised almost widely and his most recent books are *Windfall, Australian Ravens* (Puncher &

Wattmann) and *After Han Shan* (Flying Islands).

CHRIS MANSELL's experimental *101 Quads* came out this year with Puncher & Wattmann/Thorny Devil Press as the first in their visual poetics series. The book, and visual works based on it, were then shown in her exhibition (Words Becoming) at WordXImage Gallery. Another more narrative work, was also published this year, *Foxline* (Flying Islands Press). This book was prompted by seeing 200 dead foxes strung up by their ankles on a fenceline just out of Castlemaine, Victoria. Here the two main characters deal with their sense of displacement and their connection with each other and the land, sometimes in dialogue, sometimes in their own singular voices. Chris Mansell has won a number of awards, has had more than a dozen books of poetry out, and is publisher at PressPress, (possibly the smallest press in the known universe).

LIZZ MURPHY writes between Binalong NSW and Canberra ACT, a habit which began while commuting by bus (aeons ago). She has published thirteen books. Her ninth poetry title *The Wear of My Face* will be published by Spinifex Press in 2021. Other poetry titles include: *Shebird* (PressPress 2016), *Walk the Wildly* (Picaro/ Ginninderra 2009/2017), *Two Lips Went Shopping* (Spinifex Press 2000). Spinifex also published her popular anthology *Wee Girls: Women Writing from an Irish Perspective.*

DAVID MUSGRAVE teaches Creative Writing at the University of Newcastle. His most recent book is his *Selected Poems* (Eyewear, UK).

JAN OWEN is a South Australian poet and translator who has had seven books of poetry published, including *Poems 1980 – 2008*, John Leonard Press, 2008, and *The Offhand Angel*, Eyewear Publications, 2015. She received the Philip Hodgins Memorial Award for 2016. Her translations of Baudelaire's *Les Fleurs du*

Mal were published by Arc Publications in 2015.

MOYA PACEY published her third collection *Doggerland* with Recent Work Press in 2020. Both of her previous poetry collections – *Black Tulips* (Recent Work Press) and *The Wardrobe* – were shortlisted for the ACT Writers Centre Poetry Award, and she published *One Last Border: poetry for refugees* (Ginninderra Press) with Sandra Renew and Hazel Hall. Her poems have been anthologised, and most recently published in *Canberra Times, Blue Nib, London Grip, Burrow, Fem Asia, Axon, Cicerone Journal, ARTEMISPoetry UK, Meniscus, Terrain, Silence Anthology* (University of Canberra) and longlisted in 2019 for the University of Canberra International Poetry Competition. She is a founding editor of the women's online poetry journal *Not Very Quiet*. In October 2018, she was Poet in Residence at the Elizabeth Bishop House in Great Village, Nova Scotia, Canada. She has an MA in Creative and Life Writing from Goldsmiths College, University of London.

GEOFF PAGE is based in Canberra and has published twenty-four collections of poetry as well as two novels and five verse novels. His recent books include *Elegy for Emily: a verse biography* (Puncher & Wattmann) and *In medias res* (Pitt Street Poetry). He also won the 2020 Australian Catholic University Prize for Poetry. He reviews Australian poetry extensively and has run monthly poetry readings and jazz concerts in Canberra for many years.

ANITA PATEL's collection of poetry, *A Common Garment* (Recent Work Press), was published in 2019. Her work also appears in publications such as *Mascara Literary Review, Cordite Poetry Review, Plumwood Mountain Journal* and *Australian Poetry Anthology Vol. 8*. Her poetry was selected for and published in *Australian Book Review's* States of Poetry ACT.

PHYLLIS PERLSTONE, first an artist and experimental filmmaker, turned to poetry in 1992, studied at the New School for Social Research, New York. Awards include: the NSW Women Writers Poetry Prize 2004; second in the National Women Writers Poetry Prize 2005. She has published poems, reviews and articles in leading journals and anthologies – *Motherlode, Australian Love poems, Writing to the Wire, Newcastle Poetry Prize Anthology*, and *Contemporary Australian Poetry (2016)*. Her books are: *You Chase After Your Likeness* (2002), *The Edge of Everything* (2007), shortlisted for the Kenneth Slessor Prize in 2008 Premier's Award NSW; *Thick and Thin Lines* (2012), *The Bruise of Knowing* (2014). *But Now*, is to be published this year.

FELICITY PLUNKETT is a poet and critic. She is the author of *A Kinder Sea* (UQP, 2020), *Seastrands* (Vagabond Press, 2011) and *Vanishing Point* (UQP, 2009), and the editor of *Thirty Australian Poets* (UQP, 2011).

SANDRA RENEW is published in Australia in *Griffith Review, Canberra Times, Hecate, Axon, Australian Poetry Journal*. Her poetry collections are *It's the sugar, Sugar*, Recent Work Press, 2021; *Acting Like a Girl*, Recent Work Press, 2019; and *The Orlando Files*, Ginninderra Press, 2018. Sandra's collection, *Acting Like a Girl*, Recent Work Press, 2019, won the 2020 ACT Writing and Publishing Award for Poetry.

CAROLYN RICKETT is the Dean of Learning and Teaching, senior lecturer, researcher and creative arts practitioner at Avondale University. Utilising her background in arts, medical humanities and healthcare chaplaincy, she currently teaches undergraduate students and supervises postgraduate students in the fields of communication, creative writing, education, nursing and chaplaincy. She is the coordinator for *The New Leaves* writing project, and has co-edited several poetry anthologies with Judith

Beveridge, Jean Kent and David Musgrave. Her passion for poetry along with her experiences working in palliative care and hospital contexts are the inspiration for the anthology *This Gift, This Poem.*

ROBYN ROWLAND has 14 books, 11 poetry. *Under This Saffron Sun − Safran Güneşin Altında,* Knocknarone Press, Ireland 2019 and *This Intimate War Gallipoli/*Çanakkale *1915 − İçli Dışlı Bir Savaş: Gelibolu/*Çanakkale *1915* republished Spinifex Press, 2018 are bilingual; Turkish translations by Mehmet Ali Çelikel. *Mosaics from the Map,* Doire Press, Ireland 2018. Her poetry appears in national/international journals, over forty anthologies, eight editions of *Best Australian Poems.* She has read in India, Portugal, Ireland, UK, USA, Greece, Austria, Bosnia, Serbia, Turkey and Italy. She reads for *National Irish Poetry Reading Archive,* James Joyce Library, UCD, on *YouTube.* https://robynrowland.com/

PATRICIA M SAAR was born in Melbourne and trained as a nurse before moving to Sydney, bringing up her family and working in the operating theatres. Thirty years later, she attended university to upgrade her qualifications, and after that to study history. She is a member of the *New Leaves* writing group.

MELINDA SMITH is a poet, editor, teacher and performer. Her latest book is *Man-handled* (Recent Work Press, 2020). She is the author of seven other poetry books, including the 2014 Prime Minister's Literary Award winner, *Drag down to unlock or place an emergency call,* and her work has been widely anthologised and translated. She is a former poetry editor of *The Canberra Times,* and lives and writes on unceded Ngunnawal Country.

SHANE STRANGE's writing has appeared in various print and online journals in Australia and internationally. He is the author of two chapbooks, *Notes to the Reader* and *Dark Corner*. His first collection of poetry *All Suspicions Have Been Confirmed* was released in late 2020. He was Festival Director of the Poetry on the Move poetry festival from 2018-2020 and is publisher at Recent Work Press.

PATRICIA SYKES is an award-winning poet and a librettist. Her collaborations with composer Liza Lim have been performed in Australia, the UK, Germany, Moscow, Paris and New York. She was Asialink writer in Residence, Malaysia 2006. Her most recent collection is *Among the Gone of It*, (English/Chinese, *Flying Island Books*, 2017). A song cycle by Andrew Aronowicz, based on her collection *The Abbotsford Mysteries (Spinifex Press, 2011)* premiered in May 2019. A podcast is forthcoming.

ANDREW TAYLOR has published sixteen collections of poetry, the most recent being *Collected Poems* (Salt UK 2004), *The unhaunting* (Salt 2009) and *Impossible Preludes* (Margaret River Press 2016). Since leaving Perth in 2014 he divides his time between Sydney and Wiesbaden in Germany.

GILLIAN TELFORD, a NSW poet, has three published collections: *Moments of Perfect Poise* (Ginninderra Press 2008); *An Indrawn Breath* (Picaro Press 2015); and *Midnight Lexicon*, a Picaro Poets chapbook (Ginninderra Press 2020). Her work is widely published in journals and anthologies including *A Slow Combusting Hymn* (ASM & Cerberus Press, 2014); *Falling and Flying, Poems on Aging*, (Brandl & Schlesinger 2015); *Not Very Quiet*, Issues 2-4, 2018/9; and *Grieve Anthologies* (HunterWriters Centre 2016-18, 2020).

RICHARD KELLY TIPPING's books include *Instant History* (Flying Island, 2017), *Tommy Ruff* (PressPress, 2014) and the visual poetry collection *Fresh Concrete* (Puncher & Wattmann, 2021). He is known internationally for his 'artpoems' and public literary sculpture. Originally from Adelaide, after many years in Sydney and Newcastle he has recently opened a text-art gallery in the historic town Maitland, NSW. See more at www. wordximage.art

MARK TREDINNICK's latest book, his fourth collection, is *Walking Underwater* (Pitt Street Poetry, 2021*)*. Mark's twenty other books include *A Gathered Distance*, *Almost Everything I Know*, *Bluewren Cantos*, *Fire Diary*, *The Blue Plateau*, and *The Little Red Writing Book*. In 2020, he launched the online poetry masterclass *What the Light Tells*. Mark is the father of five, and he lives with his partner Jodie Williams, their spaniel Dante and their cat Sappho, in Gundungurra country, along the Wingecarribee, southwest of Sydney.
For more: marktredinnick.com.

TODD TURNER is an Australian poet who lives and works in Sydney. His first collection of poetry *Woodsmoke* was published by Black Pepper Publishing in 2014. The book was shortlisted for the Dame Mary Gilmore Award. His second collection, *Thorn*, was published by Puncher and Wattmann in 2020.

JULIE WATTS is a Western Australian writer. She has been published in national and international journals and anthologies. She won the 2018 Dorothy Hewett Award for an Unpublished Manuscript and her second poetry collection, *Legacy*, was published by UWA Publishing in November 2018.

CHRIS WALLACE-CRABBE is a widely-published Melbourne poet, an Emeritus Professor at Melbourne University and quite a healthy old chap. His latest book of poetry is *Rondo* (Carcanet, London, 2019).

JEN WEBB is Distinguished Professor of Creative Practice at the University of Canberra, and co-editor of the literary journal *Meniscus* and the scholarly journal *Axon: Creative Explorations.* She researches and writes about creativity and resilience. Her most recent poetry collections are *Moving Targets* (Recent Work Press, 2018), and *Flight Mode* (with Shé Hawke; (Recent Work Press 2020).

ANNAMARIA WELDON's latest poetry book, *Stone Mother Tongue (UWAP October 2018)*, features her birth island Malta's Stone-age Goddess culture. Weldon's earlier book with UWAP, *The Lake's Apprentice* (2014), includes poetry, nature essays and photographs of Lake Clifton Thrombolites and Western Australia's SW bushland. Previous collections are *The Roof Milkers* (Sunline Press, 2008) and *Ropes of Sand* (Associated News Malta, 1984). Annamaria is writing memoir using poetry, prose, photos and handwritten letters collected since her travels began as a child in the 1950s. In 1984 she came to Western Australia and this year is Patron of Perth Poetry Festival (September 2021).

JANE WILLIAMS is the author of several books of poems and has read her poems widely in Australia, parts of Europe, Southeast Asia, the USA and Canada. In 2016 she was awarded a three-month residency in Slovakia where she worked on poems toward her sixth collection *Parts of the Main.* Her most recent collections are *Points of Recognition* (Ginninderra Press, Australia) and *Between Breaths* (Silver Bow Publishing, Canada). She lives in Tasmania with her partner Ralph Wessman.

KIMBERLY WILLIAMS is the author of two poetry books, *Sometimes a Woman* (Recent Work Press,) and *Finally, the Moon* (Stephen F Austin University Press). She has an MFA in Creative Writing from the University of Texas El Paso. Kimberly was short-listed for the University of Canberra's Vice-Chancellor's Poetry Prize in 2019, and her poems appear in many journals and anthologies around the world. After twenty years of writing and teaching in the U.S. Southwest, Kimberly moved to Canberra to work on a PhD. She is originally from Detroit, Michigan.

Acknowledgements

Judith Beveridge's 'To a Garland Maker' was previously published in *The Weekend Australian*.

Peter Boyle's poem 'Paralysis' was originally published in *What the Painter Saw in our Faces* (Five Islands Press, 2001).

Lisa Brockwell's poem 'The Shower Stall' was previously published in the Australian Catholic University Poetry Prize Anthology.

Andrew Burke's 'Reverse Haibun' appeared in *Australian Poetry Anthology* Vol.7, 2019 and in his collection *NEW & SELECTED* (Walleah Press 2020).

Josephine Clarke's 'Our mothers, the trees' was published in *Recipe for Risotto* (UWA Publishing, 2020).

Jan Dean's 'Cranes fly on my porcelain brooch' was published in *Mascara Literary Review*, January, 1, 2011.

Ross Donlon's 'Netball in Newlyn' appears in *The Poets' Republic* (U.K.)

Robert Edmonds' 'Lingering' was previously published in *Gravity Doesn't Always Work* (Flying Islands Press 2021) (available through the author).

Theodore Ell's 'Sun-shower' was selected for publication in *The Weekend Australian – Review*. It will be published in 2021 but the date is not yet known.

Brook Emery's 'Rain as it is' was published in his book *Collusion* (JLP, 2012).

Luke Fischer's 'On the Organic Form of Art' was first published in *Philosophy, Activism, Nature* 15 (2020), pp. 64-66.

John Foulcher's 'Dancing with Stephen Hawking' was first published in *Australian Book Review* (2019) and in *Dancing with Stephen Hawking* (Pitt Street Poetry 2021).

Jennifer Harrison's 'Spring, Oxfam Brochure and Other Gifts' is from *Folly & Grief* (Black Pepper, Melbourne 2006).

Dennis Haskell's poem was first published in his collection *And Yet...* (WA Poets Publishing, 2020).

Daniel Ionita's 'Destinies' was published in a slightly different version in the volume *ContraDiction* (second edition PIM Publishing, 2017).

Ivy Ireland's 'Acorn' is from *The Owl Inside* (Puncher & Wattmann, 2020).

Jean Kent's 'The Spaghetti Maker' is from *The Satin Bowerbird* (Hale &

Iremonger, 1998.)

Andy Kissane's 'A Personal History of Joy' is from *The Tomb of the Unknown Artist* (Puncher & Wattmann, 2019).

Shari Kocher's 'Breath' is from *Foxstruck and Other Collisions* (Puncher & Wattmann, 2020).

Andrew Lansdown's 'The Homecoming' was published in *Quadrant*, 2020.

Penelope Layland's 'Uncut Pages' was first published in *Nigh* (Recent Work Press 2020).

Win Luben's poem 'Autumn' was previously published in *New Leaves Anthology* (Darlington Press, 2008).

Chris Mansell's 'Morning Frost' was published in *Spine Lingo* (Kardoorair Press, 2011).

Lizz Murphy's poem 'The Unseen River' was selected by the Poetry and Poetics Centre Committee, University of South Australia as one of five poems entered in the 2008 Max Harris Poetry Prize 'considered to be of high quality and worthy of recognition' and published on their website with winning and placed poems. In 2010 it was translated into Bengali by Mihir Chrakroboty and published in the Calcutta magazine *Nandimukh*.

Jan Owen's 'Zachary and the Angel' is from her collection *Poems 1980 – 2008* (John Leonard Press, 2008).

Moya Pacey's 'Fishing with Seamus' was previously published in *Live Encounters Poetry & Writing*, Australia New Zealand, May 2021.

Phyllis Perlstone's poem 'The Travel of Air' will be included in her collection *But Now* later in 2021.

Felicity Plunkett's 'One for sorrow' was first published in *Westerly* 65.1.

Sandra Renew's 'Three hares' was previously published in *Haibun Today*, Volume 9, Number 3, September 2015 (on-line).

Carolyn Rickett's poem 'Sweet Peas' was first published in *New Leaves Anthology* (Darlington Press, 2008).

Robyn Rowland's 'Who if I cried out ...' was first published in *The Blue Nib*, Issue 44, December 2020.

Patricia M Saars' 'New Roots, New Beginnings' was published in *New Leaves Anthology* (Darlington Press, 2008).

Melinda Smith's 'Afternoon at La Pietra' is from *Man-handled* (Recent Work Press, 2020).

Shane Strange's 'The chapel astronomer' was previously published in *All Suspicions Have Been Confirmed*, 2020, Recent Work Press.

Patricia Sykes' 'Butterflies Twice Landed' is from *Among the Gone of It* (English/Chinese, Flying Island Books, 2017).

Gillian Telford's 'Solace' is from *Moments of Perfect Poise* (Ginninderra Press, 2008).

Richard Tipping's 'Writing on Electrons' was previously published in *Southerly*.

Todd Turner's 'Grace' was previously published in *Meanjin*, Volume 68 no. 1, Autumn 2009; and in his collection *Woodsmoke* (Black Pepper Publishing, 2014).

Julie Watts' 'Floating Backwards' was published in *Legacy* by UWA Publishing in 2018.

Jen Webb's poem 'Da Capo' was previously published in her 2016 collection, *Sentences from the Archives* (Recent Work Press.)

Annamaria Weldon's poem 'Leaning backwards with Great Aunt Natalie' was first published (in a different version) in her collection *Stone Mother Tongue* (UWAP 2018).

Jane Williams' poem 'On World Heart Day' was previously published in *Parts of the Main* (Ginninderra Press 2017).

www.ingramcontent.com/pod-product-compliance
Lightning Source LLC
Chambersburg PA
CBHW030827090426
42737CB00009B/911